FromVENUS toMARS andBACK

FROM VENUS TO MARS AND BACK

What It Means to Be You

Angus N. Hunter

DESTINY IMAGE® PUBLISHERS, INC.
P.O. Box 310, Shippensburg, PA 17257-0310

"Speaking to the Purposes of God for This Generation and for the Generations to Come."

This book and all other Destiny Image, Revival Press, MercyPlace, Fresh Bread, Destiny Image Fiction, and Treasure House books are available at Christian bookstores and distributors worldwide.

For a U.S. bookstore nearest you, call **1-800-722-6774.**

For more information on foreign distributors, call **717-532-3040.**

Reach us on the Internet: **www.destinyimage.com.**

ISBN 10: 0-7684-3117-4

ISBN 13: 978-0-7684-3117-9

For Worldwide Distribution, Printed in the U.S.A.

1 2 3 4 5 6 7 8 9 10 11 / 13 12 11 10 09

DEDICATION

TO my dear Clare and our four marvelous sons, Zellyn, Trent, Delvyn, and Reeve, and their beautiful and enchanting wives. Ah yes!—and to future grandchildren! May you always continue the journey higher up and further in to Father's love and so come to know the great joy of all you were created to be and do.

ACKNOWLEDGMENTS

WITH grateful thanks…

To the many people (and students) all over the world whose friendship and encouragement have helped me to write this book. I would like to thank Beth Whittington and Mark Peterson for practical help and prayerful guidance in getting this book to the publishers. Thank you to Julia Dyer who helped in the early days with her editing skills and encouragement. Thank you to Joe and Becky Kirby not only for doing the major editorial work and giving helpful feedback, but more especially for their faithful support and invaluable friendship over the years. And finally, thank you to the team at Destiny Image for their helpful encouragement and work in getting this book out where it belongs.

ENDORSEMENTS

When God made you, He made you in His image. He made you male or female. And there is a reason. Angus Hunter explores and reveals the reason God made you who you are. Your identity. Your purpose. Your wholeness and freedom. Don't pass up this opportunity to understand the purposes of God.

—Floyd McClung
International Director of All Nations and author of numerous books
including *The Father Heart of God* and *Living on the Devil's Doorstep*

Thank you, Gus, for this masterly work on the mystery of gender which you have already taught and ministered to many of our students around the world with great effect. It is very timely and opens the way for healing and freedom for all who desire it.

—Dr. Bruce Thompson
International Dean Emeritus, College of Counseling and Health Care,
University of the Nations

What I find so fascinating about this book is its combination of biblical metaphors with its sure therapeutic touch. The combination of metaphors constitutes the mystery, your own willingness to listen to the Spirit and do as instructed, the healing. We all long to know as we are known, but the order is crucial: until we are willing to be known, which means the exposure of the truth about ourselves, we cannot know the grace which is inseparable from it. As we realize the limitlessness of grace, we realize also that nothing less would have been sufficient. As I read I felt as the disciples must have felt when Jesus said to them that kings and prophets had longed to hear what you are hearing—the revelation of the mystery of the Kingdom: a power and its use that freed and healed and ultimately perfected rather than one that dominated and destroyed. Are we ready for either that physical or spiritual intimacy?

—The Rt. Rev. Dr. Calvin Cook
Professor Emeritus, Rhodes University
Grahamstown, Republic of South Africa

It is a privilege to commend my friend Gus Hunter's unusual, compelling, important, and deeply relevant book. Not only does the volume address a critically fundamental and tender area of human life, namely our sexuality as male and female, but it does so both with deep sensitivity and compassion born out of years of experience as a much sought-after counselor and also with profound theological insight. This insight considers not only the nature of God as male and female, but also the consequent nature of humans reflecting the very image of God in our sexual make-up. In an age of pain, brokenness, and confusion about sexual identity, male/female roles, sexual morality, and even the very nature of marriage, parenting, and family life, this volume is a "must-read" for pastors, counselors, parents, and all believers who want to manage their sexuality maturely, creatively, wisely, and according to the Divine Intent. I believe there is major blessing here, and even healing, for all and any who will be brave and wise enough to absorb what Gus is here giving us.

—Michael Cassidy
Founder of Africa Enterprise and author of numerous books including
Bursting the Wine Skins and *A Passing Summer*

I have known Gus Hunter for almost 20 years and still have not met anyone like him. He has an extraordinary sensitivity to the Holy Spirit which is powerfully reflected in this book. It distills the very essence of the life that Jesus died to give us, stripping away the corrosion and corruption that Western thought has lain over the simplicity of the Gospel. Every believer needs to read this book. And if every unbeliever were to read it, they would be tearing down the doors of the church to get in!

—David Kyle Foster
Pure Passion TV

For through the law I died to the law
so that I might live for God.
I have been crucified with Christ and I no longer live,
but Christ lives in me.
The life I live in the body,
I live by faith in the Son of God,
who loved me and gave Himself for me.
I do not set aside the grace of God,
for if righteousness could be gained through the law,
Christ died for nothing!

Galatians 2:19-21

TABLE OF CONTENTS

FOREWORD

*God created man in His own image, in the image of God He
created him; male and female He created them. God blessed them
and said to them, "Be fruitful and increase in number…"*

—Genesis 1:27-28

GOD'S original intent is threefold. First, He desired that we would know that we are loved by God and that by creating us He has initiated out of love and desire for us and toward us.

Second, God wants us to have security and identity in whom He has made us to be. In creating us specifically male and female, He gives us uniqueness, security, and delight in how He has made us and how we express love to Him, to one another, and to the world around us. He created us for blessing. Since sin has entered the world, many times we live with a sense of inadequacy, inferiority, and a fear of not being loved or wanted by anyone, let alone God. This is ironic because just as a loving human father delights to bless his children, not merely to accept them but to lavish love on them, so God's original intent is to lavish blessing on His children.

Third, we see that God has created us with purpose. The three biggest questions that people ask in life are: "Who is God?" "Who am I?" and "What is His purpose for my life?" God answered all those questions in this original passage. In the presence of the Lord, apart from sin, Adam

17

and Eve lived in that reality, but this was to be short-lived. When they went their own way, they were blinded and marred by sin. Immediately, they began to ask: "Does God really love me?" "Who am I and how do I relate to the world around me?" "I wonder if God really does have a purpose for my life."

As I look at these initial three chapters of Genesis, I see God's original intent, the problem of sin, and then I see God's answer. God's answer for humanity is to bring us back to that place of original intent, and that is a journey for all of us. The God who initiated our creation is also the God who initiates our deliverance from the complexities of sin and how it has blinded us to His goodness. I like to say it this way:

God's Initiative of Love + Our Response = Our Destiny in God

By learning to respond to God out of who He has made us to be, to hear His voice, and then to respond to Him wholeheartedly, we walk out of darkness and into light. We have the opportunity to live the way God originally intended: in His presence, full of love and satisfaction in the way that He has made us, and full of purpose and destiny for which He has created us.

It is these basic truths that are life transforming for those who see them and believe them. Gus Hunter has been raised up in the Body of Christ as one who sees—one who hears and sees God's heart. For the past 15 years we have had the privilege of watching people in our church community and in the Body of Christ at large be healed, strengthened, helped, and empowered by Gus's message of responding to God out of whom He has made them to be.

In the pages you are about to read, you will be both encouraged and challenged with fresh insight on how to live a life of absolute abandoned love for God and to rightly see how He loves you and how He has made you uniquely male and female, masculine and feminine. When this journey of mystery is brought into light there, will be fresh freedom to love God and live a life of love and satisfaction with God and the people He has brought into your life.

Gus has lived a life of desiring nothing more than to love God, hear His voice, and respond to Him wholeheartedly. His passionate pursuit of hearing and responding to God above all else has brought Gus tremendous revelation in the area of finding identity in Christ. It has also allowed Gus to be used as a counselor to bring healing and restoration to people's lives through the insights that he receives from listening and responding to God on behalf of others.

We have cried together and laughed together as we have pursued these basic truths that you are about to read regarding the unique ways in which God moves in and through people. May you be set free to love God more and to be the unique person He created you to be. May this lead to greater intimacy than you have experienced before with God and with one another.

In His Strength and Love,
Jimmy Seibert
Senior Pastor, Antioch Community Church
President, Antioch Ministries International

PREFACE

THIS book had its beginnings on the north side of the Big Island of Hawaii. I was there to teach at Youth with a Mission's University of the Nations. During a break from teaching I went to Kailua Kona about 50 miles away, and spent the weekend in an apartment that a friend had offered to me. I anticipated and cherished the solitude of being alone with some good reading.

For some years I had made it a spiritual discipline to pray about the books I read and had frequently experienced the leading of the Holy Spirit as to which books I should choose. Apart from the desire to be led by God, there are so many books to read, and since I read rather slowly, I prefer to be prayerful about what I read. On this occasion, I had an intuition that God wanted me to read something in particular. I prayed and sensed God saying that I was to read not one but two books and that they would go together. I had a familiar feeling of excitement and anticipation that God was about to teach me something new.

This idea of reading two books together had never occurred to me before. I felt this was rather odd and wondered if I was really hearing Him right. I decided to go along with it in faith. My next question was to ask which two books I was to read. As I prayed and listened I had the sense from Him that I was to look for one book in the library were I was staying at the YWAM base at Makapala and that I would find the other book at my weekend destination about 50 miles south in Kailua. As I glanced through the books in the library I found *Crises in Masculinity* by Leanne Payne. As I browsed through the book it did not seem like the kind of book I would normally like, but nonetheless I felt that this was the book God wanted me to read. After I arrived at my new destination in Kona I found a bookshelf in the sitting room and began to look for the "other book." When my eyes came upon an old hardcover copy of *Perelandra,* I sensed God saying that that was the book I was to read. I had never seen or heard of it before. I was encouraged to note that it was by C.S. Lewis. I had read the *Chronicles of Narnia* to my boys and enjoyed *Mere Christianity* and *Surprised by Joy,* all of which I had relished. At a preliminary browse, I was a little disappointed in that the book seemed to be some kind of science fiction story. I was not particularly a fan of science fiction. Anyway, off I went with my two books…

I lay on my bed and settled in for a good read. I prayed about which book to read first. The answer was *Crises in Masculinity*. As I waded through the first few chapters I began to notice an extraordinary thing. I was amazed to find that in the writing of the book Leanne Payne made many references to another book—*Perelandra!* I began to realize that I had experienced a significant miracle. God had led me to two books to be read "together," and the one was to a large extent influenced by the other. When I thought about all the books in the world and considered the unlikely odds that these two books were a mere coincidence, I realized that I was beginning an extraordinary adventure with Jesus through the Holy Spirit. I had that marvelous sense that I was on the brink of something of great import.

Reading these two books began to challenge and change the narrow traditional views of gender and sexuality I had grown up with and in some ways had been held prisoner by. Had I not experienced a clear miracle in the selection of these books and with it an extraordinary sense of His presence, I would have been suspect of what I was reading and likely remained a prisoner of the prejudices passed down to me by my elders. This change in thinking created a huge paradigm shift for me. It took two to three years of careful prayer and meditation before I was able to speak about and teach the things I believe God had begun to show me.

This book is an attempt to pass on the things I learned over those years. I do not in any way think that I have dealt adequately with the material, and I imagine that there are a lot of people who could have done a far better job than me. Nonetheless here it is, and I pray that it will be an opener for more meaningful thought and an opportunity for further revelation and healing on the subject of *From Venus to Mars and Back.*

> *For this reason I kneel before the Father, from whom His whole family in heaven and on earth derives its name. I pray that out of His glorious riches He may strengthen you with power through His Spirit in your inner being, so that Christ may dwell in your hearts through faith. And I pray that you, being rooted and established in love, may have power, together with all the saints, to grasp how wide and long and high and deep is the love of Christ, and to know this love that surpasses knowledge—that you may be filled to the measure of all the fullness of God. Now to Him who is able to do immeasurably more than all we ask or imagine, according to His power that is at work within us, to Him be glory in the church and in Christ Jesus throughout all generations, for ever and ever! Amen* (Ephesians 3:14-21).

Chapter One

FOR THIS REASON

This is the written account of Adam's line. When God created
man, He made him in the likeness of God. He created them male
and female and blessed them. And when they were created,
He called them "man."

—Genesis 5:1-2

CREATED IN THE IMAGE OF GOD

WHEN God first created man and woman, both in His image, His plan was and still is to live with them in an eternal relationship of love, friendship, and unity—encompassing both the relationship of a Father with His children and the relationship of a Husband with His wife. His plan was to collaborate with them and enable them to populate and rule the earth with His justice and to fill it with His goodness and His love—in other words, all the goodness of Heaven reflected on earth in humanity.

Genesis 1:27 tells us: *"God created man in His own image, in the image of God He created him; male and female He created them."*

It is important to see that creating humankind in the image and likeness of God included creating male and female with the capacity to have children and create families that would populate the earth. It is obvious and logical to conclude that God's idea of mankind being created "in His image" included the elements that make up our sexuality. Before anything else is mentioned—free will, intelligence, feelings, imagination, or the ability to choose—this idea of being "male and female" in the image of God is announced loud and clear! This suggests to us that the idea of sexuality that exists in the mind of the eternal Father has a primary and foundational influence in shaping the lives and identities of men and women. Our identity as creatures "created in God's image" is profoundly and deeply wrapped up in our being male and female. It is also clear and intriguing that our being male and female has much to do with the very image and likeness of God Himself.

In the first two verses of chapter 5 of Genesis it is written:

> *This is the written account of Adam's line. When God created man, He made him in the likeness of God. He created them male and female and blessed them. And when they were created, He called them "man"* (Genesis 5:1-2).

It is important to note the poetic play on words in this passage. The first reference to man being created in the image of God is in the singular: *"...He made **him** in the likeness of God."* The next sentence switches to the plural: *"He created **them** male and female...."* Then God combines the plural into the singular and states a profound mystery: *"...when **they** were created, He called them **'man.'**"* It is as if we are to see the man and the woman as "one" and that "one man" as being in the image of God "male and female." (The word *Adam* in Hebrew means "a human being, the species of mankind.")

In the second chapter of Genesis there is a wonderful account of Eve being created from a rib God takes from the side of Adam. The important thing here is to see the "picture" of what is occurring. The visual impact of the story is very much part of the word of God to us. Imagine this being put into a movie. Here we have a picture of the man at first on his own. He names all the animals, but for him no suitable helper is to be found. This, apparently, is not good! Then, in verse 21…

> *So the Lord God caused the man to fall into a deep sleep;*
> *and while he was sleeping, He took one of the man's ribs*
> *and closed up the place with flesh. Then the Lord God*
> *made a woman from the rib He had taken out of the man,*
> *and He brought her to the man. The man said, "This is*
> *now bone of my bones and flesh of my flesh; she shall be*
> *called 'woman,' for she was taken out of man"* (Genesis
> 2:21-23).

In this passage, the word for *rib* in Hebrew is the same as the word for "side of." In this story or "movie," we see God reaching into the "side" of the man and taking out a rib from which He makes the woman. On seeing this, Adam exclaims, *"She will be called woman for she was taken out of man"* (Gen. 2:23). He got the picture. Woman was taken out of man! Adam said, *"Bone of my bones and flesh of my flesh!"* (Gen. 2:23). She came from the man! *Somehow, the "ingredients" of the woman were there all along.* At this very moment, the next verse tells us, *"For this reason a man will leave his father and mother and be united to his wife, and they will become one flesh."* The idea of becoming "one flesh" indicates the biblical "act of marriage" in which the man and the woman unite sexually. The phrase *"For this reason" indicates that they were one to begin with.* God is one! And *for this reason* they are to celebrate and complete the whole image of their Creator.

REPRODUCING THE IMAGE

So, in the "act of marriage," the man and the woman becoming one flesh is a celebration of the image of God. This is a significant part of the meaning of our being created male and female. Furthermore, it is also significant that God designed this moment of union to be the time at which children (who, I might remind you, are themselves created in the image of God) are conceived. It is when the man and the woman become one that we have the beginnings of family. It is only when the *whole image* is present that the "image of God" can be reproduced. The man on his own or the woman on her own cannot do it. It is only as they celebrate the whole of who God is in the act of marriage that they are able to reflect the magical[1] mystery and wonder of the person of God and in doing so reproduce that image and create a family.

This symbolic picture of a family, rather than an individual, may well be a more accurate and more complete picture of what it means to be created in the image of God. After all, He did say, "Let *Us* create man in *Our* image" and not "Let *Me* create man in *My* image." God is Himself a mysterious unity, a "family" of Father, Son, and Holy Spirit.

It is the substance and nature of God that He is love and that He must love. Therefore it is impossible that He should be alone. There are some things that are impossible even for God! It is impossible for God not to be God. As God He would be a Father and He would have children. The nature of God is imaged into the creation of the man and the woman. It is more fully expressed when they come together in the loving act of marriage in order to fill the world with a family of children who can in turn be loved and, in being loved, learn to love. I can imagine God being eternally enthused about this wonderful idea. After all, personality only comes about through relationship and unity.

EPHESIANS 5

All the work of Creation was simply God's love exploding out of Him in a vast and splendid expression of who He is, reaching a final and exquisite crescendo in the creation of Adam and Eve as His son and daughter. Both of these children together deeply and intimately express varied aspects of the one true image and nature of the Father who created them. The capacity to celebrate being one and to have children is very much part of God's pattern and plan!

There is a fabulous passage in Ephesians 5:21-32 that parallels the story of Adam and Eve. It begins with, *"Submit to one another out of reverence for Christ"* (Eph. 5:21). It then speaks of wives submitting to their husbands as the Church submits to Christ and of husbands loving their wives as Christ loves the Church. At the end of the passage, Paul concludes with this quote from Genesis, *"For this reason a man will leave his father and mother and be united to his wife, and the two will become one flesh"* (Eph. 5:31). He adds, *"This is a profound mystery—but I am talking about Christ and the church"* (Eph. 5:32). In reference to a man and a woman uniting and becoming one flesh, he indicates that he is talking about Christ and the Church! Somehow the picture of sexual unity is here used as a symbolic picture of the relationship between Christ and the Church. I love Paul's declaration that this is a profound mystery. May we be freed from our fallen nature which leads us to reduce all mysteries to some simple explanation or even scientific formula that would presume to understand the unfathomable! What the Scriptures call a mystery should be accepted and left as such. All we can do is see and hear…and ponder these marvelous things in our hearts. Being created as sexual beings is significantly symbolic of the very identity and person of God! We are fearfully and wonderfully created in the Father's image.

SEXUALITY—A SHADOW

Understanding that humans are created in God's image does not indicate that God Himself is a sexual being as we understand it on the level of our human physiology. Although we struggle to understand the concept of sexuality apart from the physical, we acknowledge that God created sexuality. Yet we also know that God is Spirit. Moses knew that God was not really a "burning bush" although He appeared to him *in* a burning bush. And John, when writing Revelation, knew that Jesus was not physically a lion or a lamb (He is both and more!). He is infinitely more than any one physical or tangible symbol He chooses to use to represent something of Himself.

Our human sexuality is symbolic and as such creates pictures that tell us things about the nature of God. The existence of our sexuality and gender is clearly a physical gift from God to us, yet it is much more. It is also a tangible symbol, like a parable or a picture, that helps us understand deep things about God which are holy and awesome and, as Job in his repentant state said, "too wonderful to know." If this is so, then for us, our sexuality is significant and quite sacred and therefore something to be cherished and protected from the degrading and perverting influence of the enemy. Sex and gender must not be allowed to become perverted because as such it would convey distorted messages about the Creator who is altogether holy and good. The children in this world desperately need to see true and real reflections of the eternal Father in the adults about them. Alas! All is fallen and broken in more ways than we can think or imagine!

ETERNAL FATHERHOOD AND MOTHERHOOD

Fatherhood and motherhood did not begin with Adam and Eve. Parenthood, both paternal and maternal, has existed eternally and has always been integral and central to who God is! God did not suddenly come up with the idea when He created man. Parenthood, in all its various expressions of fatherhood and motherhood, has always been eternally lodged at the very heart of who God the eternal Parent is. Transcendent masculinity and femininity were essentially in God from the beginning and quite naturally found expression in the creation of most aspects of our world, including the animals and plants and especially in the creation of Adam and Eve as the first father and mother of all humans. For this reason, a man will leave his father and mother and unite with his wife and the two will become one flesh!

Just as God's attributes of love, goodness, faithfulness, kindness, righteousness, peace, beauty, and loveliness are eternal and immeasurable mysteries beyond the grasp of our limited minds, so too are the masculine and feminine aspects of who He is. All of the mysteries of eternal Fatherhood and Motherhood are wrapped up in Him and hidden in the great depths of who He is. All we have in the created world are symbols, pictures, and stories that enable us at the very least to meditate on and contemplate with our heart's imagination who God is, lest we like Job speak "of things too wonderful for us to know." It is an absurd thought that we would ever come to know Him fully. Paul in Ephesians writes of us coming "*to know this love that cannot be known*" (see Eph. 3:19).

Since we are created in His image, it is probable that we will never come to fully know and fully understand ourselves either—certainly not as

God does. When we, like Job, finally come to see that much about God and His creation is a mystery, we begin to understand the importance of poetic stories and symbolic pictures and perhaps realize why the Bible is so full of these. After all, Jesus taught mainly in parables, using simple stories to bring everyday pictures to the mind of the hearer to communicate spiritual truths that were beyond the grasp of the rational intellect.

You cannot on a rational level explain intellectually the idea of color to a blind person. You have to see "yellow" in order to know what it is, and even then you cannot explain it. There is much that cannot be measured and understood in a solely technical or scientific way. Thank God there are scientists and physicists like Einstein who acknowledged and appreciated that the more you learn the greater the mystery becomes. Reason loses its reason when it denies mystery. We need the Holy Spirit to reveal these things to us. They need to be seen, not just heard. A repentant and humbled Job finally admits, *"Up til now my ears have heard about you but now my eyes have seen you and I repent in sackcloth and ashes"* (see Job 42:5-6). It is my earnest prayer that God would give us the Spirit of wisdom and revelation so that we would know Him better!

Something to Do

Prayerfully think about the idea of seeing rather than merely hearing. What was Job repenting of when he said *"Up til now my ears have heard about you but now my eyes have seen you and I repent in sackcloth and ashes"?* Ask the Holy Spirit to help you hear and apply what He would say to you in regard to this chapter.

Endnote

1. The word *magic* is used here in the definition which denotes "wonder" and not the definition which would denote slight of hand or manipulating the supernatural. It is a wonderful word when used in reference to God, not so much when used in reference to humanity.

Chapter Two

INITIATIVE AND RESPONSE

*What springs from my self and not from God is evil: It is a
perversion of something of God's. Whatever is not of faith is sin;
it is a stream cut off—a stream that cuts itself off from its
source and thinks to run on without it.*

—George MacDonald,
Unspoken Sermons—The Inheritance

I
N contemplating the meaning of what masculinity and femininity are
in creation, perhaps the best words to use are *initiative* and *response*. If
you think of the relationship between things and, in particular, people,
it is natural to incorporate the idea of initiative and response in every interaction. Relationship, and therefore truth, cannot exist without this concept
of initiation and response. Leanne Payne says:

> One of the easiest ways to define masculine/feminine is to
> state that the essence of masculinity is initiation, of femi-
> ninity, response. The terms, masculine and feminine, must
> be understood as spiritual and as psychological principles
> as well as polar forces which can (and must, if we are to be
> whole) find expression in both man and woman.

Authority and Submission

As initiative and response relate to masculinity and femininity, so do authority and submission. Humankind has abused and misused these two words in unfortunate and perverse ways to exert control over each other. The words need redeeming!

The healthy relationship between authority and submission is a graceful creative dance, not a predetermined regimented march. God never intended humans to have a manipulative grasp for control or a domineering demand for mindless or subservient conformity. This dance between authority and submission applies not only to the relationship between men and women, but also between mother and child, doctor and patient, teacher and pupil, shopkeeper and client, and so on.

Initiation and response are parallel elements in the interaction between authority and submission. Someone, not necessarily a man, is usually in a position of authority, or initiation, and another is in a position of submission, or response. In many cases, such as that of a teacher or a doctor, it may be a woman who takes the initiative and is in the primary place of authority. If the activity is catching lizards, it may well be a child or perhaps even a cat!

In everyday life we can also see the inescapable relationship we have with the authority of natural law. The law of gravity is an obvious example. Music has its own laws of rhythm and harmony. Musicians understand that they need to submit to the intrinsic rules of music. The rules simply exist and have a natural authority. Our work is to learn to respond to these rules. Much of this is common sense.

The Greeks referred to the natural law that permeates all of creation as the *logos*, the divine reason that is within all things and that governs all things. The Chinese people call it *Tao*—the course of life and its relation to external truth. In the pursuit of truth we label different fields of study like *geology, theology,* and *psychology* using words conjugated from the Greek word *logos*, which indicates the pursuit of knowledge or truth, the logos. All learning involves intelligent examination of the natural laws inherent in the things around us. We learn to recognize that the logos or natural law has authority to which we as students must learn to submit.

Only as we submit with careful discipline do we learn to function within this authority in a healthy way and so, in turn, receive authority from the very thing (or person) we submit to. This is the natural order of things. We cannot change this. There is no democracy in the created order around us. We do not vote on the color yellow or on what a sunset ought to be. We observe, we study, we learn, and we submit and respond. This is the very essence of reality, relationship, and life. The natural logos creates or initiates a framework which we learn to respond to.

MEN AND WOMEN

The scriptural mandate that a woman should submit to her husband is a call from the Creator to the woman to respond to the natural, Creator-designed ability in a *whole* man to love and protect and lead. She is to show respect to him and let God lead him. This of course assumes the man is submitting first to God and not leading out of some fallen notion to dominate and abuse. Within marriage the man's mandate from God is that he should love his wife as Christ loves the Church and gave His life for her! This is obviously not a directive for domination, manipulation, and control. Far from it, it is a call to servanthood and to laying down one's life for the good of another.

Unfortunately there has been a great deal of incorrect and perverted interpretation of God's plan that man would have authority over woman. The authority given to the man is limited and defined! It has far more to do with taking up his cross daily and following Jesus than in being king of his castle, dominating his wife and everyone else under his control. Jesus' command and example of washing the disciples' feet is particularly applicable to the relationship of a man to his wife and his children. The Creator gives man *authority* to *love* his wife as Christ loves the Church. In God's order, the more *authority* a man has the more of a *servant* he becomes. When a man is wounded and insecure, his sense of authority can go wrong and we end up with twisted interpretations and presumptuous expressions of authority.[2] The schoolyard bully in his pursuit of power is of course the last to know, let alone admit, that he is afraid, anxious, or insecure.

WHY WE REFER TO GOD IN THE MASCULINE GENDER

The essence of fatherhood and motherhood are wrapped up in the person of God. In Him it is all one—a part of the marvelous wonder of who He is. The eternal unity of the masculine and the feminine is as much a mystery as the Trinity. God the Father, the Son, and the Holy Spirit are "One God." Just as mysterious but no less true, God is fully masculine and fully feminine and is fully father and fully mother to His children. This does not mean that we have the option of referring to God as "Mother" or "she." There is good reason for this, and it has nothing to do with the erroneous idea of superiority of men over women!

Through the centuries Bible scholars have suggested the reason for referring to God in the masculine is defined by our relationship to Him. He is the Creator who initiates and we are the created ones who respond. As God, He is in supreme authority and has set in motion the order of all things. We are empty and He fills our emptiness. We, the creatures, respond to what is. He leads and we follow.

In William P. Young's recent book *The Shack,* God reveals Himself to the main *human* character, Mack, as a rather maternal African-American woman. This was apparently a necessity since, in the story, Mack had had a rather unfortunate childhood relationship with his father which had in turn badly distorted his image of God. He needed his image of God transformed. In the story God writes Mack a message inviting him to meet in "the shack" and signs the note as "Papa." Yet, when Mack meets this Papa, he manifests Himself as an African-American woman. Mack knows this is God and yet continues referring to Him as "Papa." I think that this story wonderfully illustrates the mystery of God being both fully father and mother to His children and yet being addressed in the masculine gender—not because the masculine gender is superior but because the masculine gender is symbolic of *initiative.* God is the prime divine Initiator of all things and His creation responds! It is in this sense we rightly address God as *Papa,* even if we know quite clearly that He is wonderfully and eternally both Mama and Papa all at the same time. The imagery in Scripture of the Church as a Bride and Christ as the Bridegroom echoes the same sentiment. Inside this Bridegroom is a very real mother hen that would gather her chicks under her wing!

ADAM AND EVE

At times, Adam, the man created in God's image, is to *represent* God as the authority or initiator. The woman was taken out of man and created from him. She represents all that is creaturely—including the man! The man needs to remember that he merely *represents* the Creator and *that* only in certain respects. He must remember that he is as much a creature as the woman and, as creatures, they are equal. The relationship between Adam and Eve is a picture, a shadow of the "marriage" between God and His creatures. However Adam and Eve together, as God's children or God's creatures, are considered equal before Him. Equally precious, equally loved, equally created in His image.

Paul tells us that in Christ there is neither male nor female (see Gal. 3:28). This is not a mandate for men or women to throw away their uniqueness as sexual beings and become "sexless." Nor is it an indication that we should no longer make the effort to understand what it means to be a man or a woman. There are times when it is pertinent to function in our gender roles and there are times when it is right to put aside our gender. To learn this is an art, and it takes grace. Here, there is no easy formula.

The Church, which includes all believers, male and female, is the Bride of Christ. Christ is the Bridegroom. We, both male and female, are the "Bride" because we are all, regardless of our gender, creatures in relation to God. This is a good reason why we dare not refer to God in the feminine gender. God the Father is not a bride! If we, as creatures, refer to God in the feminine, then who takes the place of the masculine? Who gets to be the bridegroom? Is it us, the creatures? We are, in a sense, an empty space that God fills. It is not the other way around! He shines the light of who He is into us, and we receive it in joy and obedience as the eye receives light in order to see and the ear sound in order to hear. Jesus, as our human example, said that without the Father He could do nothing. It is the same for us.

Both men and women must come to terms with the ultimate and transcendent masculinity of God as the Creator and Initiator of all things. He is supreme. In the book *That Hideous Strength* by C.S. Lewis there is an interaction between the Director and Jane. Jane is quite strident in her rejection of the traditional ways of understanding herself as a woman (the bad as well as the good) in general, and in relation to her husband in particular. She has "thrown the baby out with the bath water." We take up the conversation:

> ...She took it for granted, half-unconsciously, that the Director was the most virginal of his sex; but she had not realized that this would leave his masculinity on the other side of the stream from herself and even steeper, more emphatic, of that of common men. Some knowledge of a world beyond Nature she had already gained from living in his house, and more from fear of death that night in the dingle. But she had been conceiving this world as "spiritual" in the negative sense—as some neutral, democratic, vacuum where differences disappeared, where sex and sense were not transcended but simply taken away. Now the suspicion dawned upon her that there might be differences and contrasts all the way up, richer, sharper, even fiercer at every rung of the ascent. How if this invasion of her own being in marriage from which she had recoiled, often in the very teeth of instinct, were not, as she had supposed, merely a relic of animal life or patriarchal barbarism, but rather the lowest, the first, and the easiest form of some shocking contact with reality which would have to be repeated—but in ever larger and more disturbing modes—on the highest level of all?
>
> "Yes," said the Director. "There is no escape. If it were a virginal rejection of the male, He would allow it. Such souls can by pass the male and go on to meet something

far more masculine, higher up, to which they must make an even deeper surrender. But your trouble has been with what old poets called *Daungler*. We call it pride. You are offended by the masculine itself: the loud, interruptive, possessive thing—the gold lion, the bearded bull—which breaks through hedges and scatters the little kingdom of your primness as the dwarves scattered the carefully made bed. The male you could have escaped, for it exists only on the biological level. But the masculine none of us can escape. What is above and beyond all things is so masculine that we are all feminine in relation to it. You had better agree with your adversary quickly."

"You mean I shall have to become a Christian?" said Jane.

"It looks like it," said the Director.[2]

God is redeeming us and as such is preparing us as a "Bride" for Himself. This does not mean that a man should think himself a woman or "feminine" in regard to God or Christ. It does mean that both men and women should think of themselves as living in humble submission to the loving care and leadership of Christ, a Christ who in various ways stoops to wash the feet of others. Christ is the one who initiates, and male and female alike respond. The man and woman together are equal as they stand before Him who is the ultimate and highest masculinity in the relationship dance between Creator and creatures. As Paul said, *"In Christ there is neither... male nor female..."* (Gal. 3:28).

THE SYMBOLISM OF SEXUALITY

Our creation as sexual beings, especially as it is played out in the intimacy of the act of marriage, tells the story of a higher reality in a symbolic and poetic way. We see the drama played out of the love relationship and desired intimacy between God and His children. Man, even though he is himself a mere creature, plays the part of the Creator and the woman the part of the creature. It tells the story that God and man are to be one, a story of love and the desired marriage between the Creator and His creatures.

The night before Jesus died He prayed:

> *That all of them may be one, Father, just as You are in Me and I am in You. May they also be in us so that the world may believe that You have sent Me. I have given them the glory that You gave Me, that they may be one as We are one: I in them and You in Me. May they be brought to complete unity to let the world know that You sent Me and have loved them even as You have loved Me* (John 17:21).

It is for this Jesus died. It is for this we are saved…that we should be one with God in the same way that the Son is one with the Father. It is a joy to respond to His initiative and be part of the answer to this great prayer for the restoration of life and marriage between the Creator and His creatures.

SOMETHING TO DO

Like David in Psalm 139:23-24, pray that God would search you to see if there is a way in you that needs to be changed and help you walk in the way that is eternal. *"Search me, O God, and know my heart; test me and know my anxious thoughts. See if there is any offensive way in me, and lead me in the way everlasting."* Take time to humbly listen to the Holy Spirit speak to you about your picture of God and see if there are ways of thinking that He would change so you can better understand who He is and who you are in response to Him.

ENDNOTES

1. When men are products of cultures that insist that they are chauvinistic and overly dominant, they are wounded. Such men

would often vehemently refuse the idea that they are wounded. That is part of their woundedness!

2. C.S. Lewis, *That Hideous Strength* (New York, NY: Macmillan Publishing Company, 1965).

Chapter Three

GOD AS FATHER AND MOTHER

*One of the great goods that come of having two parents is that
the one balances and rectifies the motions of the other. No one is
good but God. No one holds the truth, or can hold it, in one and
the same thought, but God. Our human life is often, at best, but an
oscillation between the extremes which together make the truth.*

—George MacDonald, *The Seaboard Parish*

CREATION AND THE CHARACTER OF GOD

IN Romans chapter 1 verses 19-20 Paul tells us that all of creation
speaks to us about who God is. Everything that God created makes the
invisible qualities of God clear to all humankind. Creation tells about
two things: His "divine character" and His "infinite power."

> *Since what may be known about God is plain to them,
> because God has made it plain to them. For since the cre-
> ation of the world God's invisible qualities—His eternal
> power and divine nature—have been clearly seen, being*

understood from what has been made, so that men are without excuse (Romans 1:19-20).

Very often, the Scriptures point to things in the created world as pictures and/or symbols to illustrate the nature and character of God. We are told that He is the Lily of the Valley, the Rock of Ages, the Bread of Life, the Water of Life, the Tree of Life, the Light of the World, the Lion, the Lamb, the Bright Morning Star, and so on. The list is as long as there are created things! It is as if every created thing tells us of some aspect of the Creator. Pictures with their symbolic meanings are as much the "word of God" as the characters that form the words on the pages of the Bible. The actual words are often like the small but significant strokes of a paint brush that serve to make a bigger picture. It is "seeing" the picture that tells us what God is saying. The Word of God to us is often symbolically contained in the stories that are told—or "painted."

At the final climax and pinnacle of all the many created things that reflect and reveal His image, God creates *man*. Man—and by *man* we mean Adam (the man and the woman together)—is the highest expression of the image of God. They are His very own children, the clearest and ultimate expression in creation of who He is.

GOD'S SIGNATURE ON CREATION

My wife's father, who is a pastor in South Africa, once had a vivid dream that was quite revealing about the story of God and His creation of the world. In the dream he saw God painting a picture. The process followed the steps of the creation story with all the different elements and species of creation being painted onto the canvas…with the exception of Adam and Eve. At the completion of the picture, God reached to the bottom corner where most artists put their signature and there He painted Adam and Eve into the picture. The man and the woman alongside each other are God's very signature on the work of creation. They carry the very name and reflect the identity of God in this world.

Foremost and most obvious in all creation is the fabulous and wonderful idea of gender. From this "painted" picture, and from what the Scriptures tell us, we see that in the making of Adam and Eve God reveals and expresses His image in both masculine and feminine form. Man is created "male and female in the image of God." He is Himself both Father and Mother to Adam and Eve and their subsequent sons and daughters!

The man expresses the masculine Fatherhood of God—that aspect of God's nature that initiates, that provides leadership and direction, structure and order. He who is the essence of love, goodness, and justice is the One who initiates with His children. The creation of the woman expresses the maternal nature of God—the responding and nurturing aspects of who God is. He is a God who is constantly responding to the various needs of His creatures, and He comes with unconditional nurturing and tender love to heal and care for His children.

The maternal "part" of the character of God says, "I simply love you; you are My child, eternally of great value to Me. Do not fear...I am with you; I will never leave you or forsake you! You are the apple of My eye. You are infinitely precious to Me." When we experience the nurturing and we fully grasp the way in which we are loved, then the Father part of the character of God says, "Little children, love one another as I have loved you. Follow Me! Go...into the entire world and preach My good news to all people. I have a journey for you to go on and things I have prepared for you to do and say...Come on! Let's do it! Put your hand to the plough! To battle!"

It is important to see the significance that, in the relationship between God and His creatures, He is generally the One who initiates and the creatures are the ones who respond. It is therefore appropriate that we mostly refer to God as *Father*, in the masculine. He is the Lord of all life and the Initiator of all things!

Similarly, even the wife of a national leader might refer to her husband in public as "Mr. President" or a husband call his wife "Mrs. Prime Minister." However, in the privacy of their home she would no doubt call him "Joe" or simply "honey," and the children would call them Daddy or

Mum. In the same way, we are able to be more intimate with the Father when we are alone with Him. There are intimate times with God where it is appropriate and even necessary to see and experience God as Mother as well as Father and receive the unconditional nurturing love and sustenance "She" would give.

It would be equally scriptural for men and women to see God as a close Friend, a Rock, an Anchor, as a Shepherd with a lamb, or as a Bridegroom with His Bride. All these pictures of Him are the word of God to us! Again, in the image of Adam and Eve we are told that He is both Father and Mother.

In Isaiah chapter 66 references God loving Israel (and "Jerusalem") as a mother loves and nurtures a child:

> *For this is what the Lord says: "I will extend peace to her like a river, and the wealth of nations like a flooding stream; you will nurse and be carried on her arm and dandled on her knees. As a mother comforts her child, so will I comfort you; and you will be comforted over Jerusalem." When you see this, your heart will rejoice and you will flourish like grass...* (Isaiah 66:12-14).

Here is a promise that tells us when we see this *maternal* aspect of God's love we will flourish as the grass! We need to see it. It needs to be revealed to us by the Holy Spirit. For this, we pray and we wait! We are told to *"Be still, and know that I am God..."* (Ps. 46:10).

A number of references in Scripture also describe God as an eagle that nurtures and trains its young. It is common knowledge that it is generally the mother bird that does this. The Scriptures have a number of references to God's care of His people expressed in this beautiful picture of the nurturing and sustaining care of the mother bird with its young.

Deuteronomy 32 verses 10-12:

> *In a desert land He found him, in a barren and howling waste. He shielded him and cared for him; He guarded him*

as the apple of His eye, like an eagle that stirs up its nest and hovers over its young, that spreads its wings to catch them and carries them on its pinions. The Lord alone led him; no foreign god was with him.

Ruth 2 verse 12:

May the Lord repay you for what you have done. May you be richly rewarded by the Lord, the God of Israel, under whose wings you have come to take refuge.

Psalm 17 verse 8:

Keep me as the apple of Your eye; hide me in the shadow of Your wings.

Psalm 36 verse 7:

How priceless is Your unfailing love! Both high and low among men find refuge in the shadow of Your wings.

Psalm 57 verse 1:

Have mercy on me, O God, have mercy on me, for in You my soul takes refuge. I will take refuge in the shadow of Your wings until the disaster has passed.

Psalm 91 verse 4:

He will cover you with His feathers, and under His wings you will find refuge; His faithfulness will be your shield and rampart.

Growing up in Africa I would sometimes have opportunity to watch a mother hen with its young chicks. The mother would lead its young about calling them here and there as she found nourishing tidbits to eat. Occasionally she would squawk and fly at a dog or cat that came too close. Her careful attention to her young was enchanting and mesmerizing. The gurgling sounds she would make, the little squawks of her carefulness were a constant reminder to the little ones of her comforting and protective presence. After a time of going about finding food she would spread her wings and annunciate a special command at which they would all come running to gather under her. She would then settle down to rest with all of her brood completely hidden under her wings. It was a time to rest, to be refreshed and renewed. I could only imagine what a soft, warm comforting place that was.

Whenever I would watch this scene, tears would always well up in my eyes as revelation flooded into me as to how the eternal Father loves and cares for His children. The Holy Spirit would speak to me of the story of my relationship with the God who loves me. The image is biblical! In the modern world many grow up in large cities and are robbed of seeing and experiencing the significance of such scenes.

Jesus had also seen the picture of the hen with her chicks. He saw it from the perspective of being God. Matthew's Gospel chapter 23 gives a reference to Jesus expressing a compassionate love and longing to gather and care for Jerusalem. Giving expressing to this deep longing from His great heart, Jesus likened Himself to a mother hen with its chicks:

> O Jerusalem, Jerusalem, you who kill the prophets and stone those sent to you, how often I have longed to gather your children together, as a hen gathers her chicks under her wings, but you were not willing (Matthew 23:37).

Of all the things in the world, there is hardly a more maternal picture He could have chosen. Here we see the work of creation speaking to us, telling us who God is in His divine, eternal, and loving nature.

EL SHADDAI

The name *El Shaddai* speaks of God the Almighty as the One who is all sufficient. It also *may* remotely refer to God as one with many breasts.

(*Shad* is a word for breast in Hebrew.) Of course, God does not literally have breasts as He is Spirit. However, God as the Almighty has within Himself the capacity and desire to nurture and love His children in a deeply maternal way—to be all sufficient. There is no connection here with the goddess Diana of Ephesus who is also known as the one with many breasts.[1] Diana is merely the pagan counterfeit of something that is true. All counterfeits are based on and are distortions of things that are true.

Martha Beck (who lived her life in an academic environment) in her book *Expecting Adam* writes of her journey into discovering motherhood in a society that is predominantly misogynistic and chauvinistic. At the time, Martha was pregnant and in great need of some good *mothering*. She found it in two friendly acquaintances who insisted on taking care of her. This kind of maternal care can be found all over our world if we look for it and are willing to receive it.

> ...the understanding that the word *mother* is more powerful when it is used as a verb than as a noun. Mothering has little to do with biological reproduction—as another friend once told me, there are women who bear and raise children without ever mothering them, and there are people (both male and female) who mother all their lives without ever giving birth. The bad news is that not all of us have the good fortune to be born to our *real* mothers,[2] or to stay with them as long as we need them. The good news is that, while mothers are often in short supply, mothering is not. Against all odds, despite everything that works against it on this unpleasant, uncomfortable planet, mothering is here in abundance. You can always find it, if you're smart and know where to look.

> Of course, while I was expecting Adam, I ended up being mothered even though I didn't have a clue where to look. Not only did I fail to go out and find people to mother me through that difficult time, I actually tried to keep them away when they showed up on their own. You have to let

down your defenses in order to be mothered, and after seven years in a culture obsessed with academic achievement, my defenses were just about the only parts of my personality I had left. Whatever force it was that brought Sibyl up to my apartment, and made her return with Deirdre the following day—and the day after that, and the day after that—was also loving enough to make sure I was too sick to send them away.[3]

SOMETHING TO DO

Ask God to show you if there are ways you have blocked receiving maternal love from Him and ask Him to help you see and receive all the ways He loves you.

ENDNOTES

1. "**Diana**." *Encyclopedia Britannica*. 2009. Encyclopedia Britannica Online. Accessed June 9 2009 from <http://www.britannica.com/EBchecked/topic/161524/Diana>.

2. A "real" mother here refers to someone who has done the real work of mothering in one's life. Sadly, this is not always one's biological mother.

3. Martha Beck, *Expecting Adam* (New York, NY: Berkley Publishing Group, 1999), 61.

Chapter Four

BRIDEGROOM AND BRIDE

He has taken me to the banquet hall, and his banner over me is
love. ...Awake, north wind, and come, south wind! Blow on
my garden, that its fragrance may spread abroad. Let my
lover come into his garden and taste its choice fruits.

—Song of Songs 2:4 and 4:16

A more difficult analogy for many to cope with is the idea in the Scriptures of seeing Jesus as a Bridegroom and the "creature" (the Church) as a Bride. It is challenging for most men to think of or see themselves in the role of Bride with the Creator. For the most part, the Song of Songs is understood not only as a direct story about two lovers but also about the relationship between God and His people. It is both, and appropriately so! How does the ordinary everyday man get to understand himself as the Bride of Christ or in the role of the "beloved" in the Song of Songs? Does he put on a dress or have his hair done and put makeup on in order to make the connection? It has nothing to do with such things!

First, we must understand that it means that God is the Initiator in the relationship, and it is our place to respond with childlike trust and obedience. Second, we must see and grasp the reality that He loves us with a great passion and longing. He wants to fill us and be one with us, and in this regard we are told that the whole story of redemption is headed for a great marriage feast. At that time there will be a celebration and consummation of the prayer that Jesus prayed in John chapter 17, the night before He died:

> *My prayer is not for them alone. I pray also for those who will believe in Me through their message, that all of them may be one, Father, just as You are in Me and I am in You. May they also be in Us so that the world may believe that You have sent Me. I have given them the glory that You gave Me, that they may be one as We are one: I in them and You in Me. May they be brought to complete unity to let the world know that You sent Me and have loved them even as You have loved Me* (John 17:20-23).

This is the very thing Jesus died for. This was the prayer the Son of God carried in His heart with great emotion the night before He was crucified. The Scriptures indicate that God has a deep passion and longing to be one with His creatures, to be in us and have us in Him. The work of salvation is not simply some technical "out-of-orderness" that has to be put right. Our salvation is a matter of infinite, relentless love and bright passion. It is with a "lovesick" heart that Christ went to the cross to do the work of salvation. The Father willed it with the same kind of love and agony. He is in all things one with His Son. It was a great longing that God and man be made one again that brought Him down to earth. He desires that our emptiness be filled with His eternal presence and life-giving goodness. He longs that the stream be connected once more with the Source!

We are told in the Bible that God would woo us to Himself as a lover woos his beloved. That He should do this despite our repeated unfaithfulness and spiritual adultery is sheer amazing grace and fantastic forgiveness. We are pursued until we are found and captivated by the eternal embrace of His intimate love and kindness.

In the Scriptures the relationship between God and His people is frequently told as a story of lovers. We are told that God's beloved people have repeatedly been unfaithful and gone after other gods "fornicating" and committing adultery. Using strong language, the Bible says we have been like a whore running every which way after the things He created rather than being devoted to the Creator who loves us. We have become spiritually one with our idols and brought upon ourselves the consequences of our actions.

GOD'S WOOING LOVE

In boundless mercy and brokenhearted love the real and true God comes pursuing His beloved, giving His very life for her in order that she should be won back to Him. All the while, as a final climax to the story of redemption, this God has a great party in mind. There is to be a marriage feast in which eternal oneness with Him in boundless love is to be celebrated in ways that are beyond anything we can think or imagine. With this joy set before Him, He went to the cross to endure the humiliation and death that would miraculously bring about our redemption. The Bible tells that He took all our wrongs on Himself and He paid the price in our place. I am reminded of a song I sang as a child:

> "O the love that drew salvation's plan...
> O the grace that brought it down to man...
> O the mighty gulf that God did span at Calvary!
> Mercy there was great and grace was free;
> Pardon there was multiplied to me;
> O the mighty gulf that God did span...
> At Calvary!"[1]

It is the Father's desire that we should be taken and swept away by this great act of love. We are to be won by His mercy and kindness and by it be empowered to love Him back and so live in His goodness. By our trust in Him, we are able to make His great heart glad by our response to the actions of this great Lover, and in so doing be filled with His goodness and holiness. Thus we are to be transformed and remade by the power of the Holy Spirit. We are wrong if we think that the mere acquisition of good doctrine is going to achieve this. We have to see this great love and kindness—it is when we see that we are transformed. It is a righteousness that is from God and comes to us by revelation and is by faith from first to last!

In our coming together with God in this "celebration of marriage," the law is fulfilled as we are caught up in a gift of righteousness that exceeds the righteousness of the law. This is not a mere man-made righteousness—a righteousness that we can call our own—it is a righteousness that springs from a fire of exquisite holiness and love that is the very presence of the living God within! It is a righteousness that is a consuming passion in which all things are healed as we are made one with the Father and His Christ. Jesus said; "If you *love* Me…you will obey Me"! Love expresses itself in obedience. Our love for Him engendered by His Spirit flows out of us and fulfills the law.

We have been created with the ability to respond to the love of God. Let the Bride say "Come!" Come Lord Jesus…Fill us with Your presence and put Your Kingdom and Your righteousness inside us. Fill us with the goodness and fiery relentless passion of Heaven. Overwhelm us and ravish us with Your love. Raise us up as Your forgiven and redeemed Bride. Put the fire of Your holiness in our bones so that we can run with the healing message of your Gospel to all the sons and daughters of Adam and Eve.

Romans chapter 8 tells us that all of creation waits in eager expectation for the sons of God to be revealed and that in time creation itself will be liberated from its bondage to decay and brought into the glorious freedom of the children of God. It all begins now! It begins with you and me, as we respond each day to this God who loves us and desires to fill us with Himself and lead us into the various and myriad dimensions of His holiness, goodness, and bright passion.

ENDNOTE

1.   William Newell (1868-1956), *At Calvary*

Chapter Five

LION AND LAMB

*"...Do not weep! See, the Lion of the tribe of Judah, the Root of
David, has triumphed. He is able to open the scroll and its seven
seals. Then I saw a Lamb..."*

—Revelation 5:5-6

*"'Please, Lamb,' said Lucy, 'is this the way to Aslan's country?'...
'There is a way into my country from all the worlds,' said the
lamb; but as he spoke his snowy white flushed into tawny gold and
his size changed and he was Aslan himself, towering above them
and scattering light from his mane."*

—C.S. Lewis, *The Voyage of the Dawn Treader*

ONE way to think about the polarity of the masculine and the feminine as it exists in the persons of the Trinity is to consider and meditate on the ways Jesus is revealed and spoken of in the Book of the Revelation. We are told He is a Lion and He is a Lamb.

In chapter 5 John is found weeping because he has been told that there is no one to be found who is worthy to break open the seals of the future.

Just then, one of the elders cries out that someone who is worthy has been found! He announces Him as "the Lion of the tribe of Judah." John goes on to say, "I looked and behold I saw a Lamb." Here the Scripture, as in most of the Book of the Revelation, is not communicating by means of discursive logic but in pictures. Here we have pure poetic pictures and symbols that speak to us of who Jesus is. He is a Lion that is a Lamb and a Lamb that is a Lion. He is mysteriously both lion and lamb all at once. These two aspects of who the Son of God is cannot be separated from each other. The one is essentially part of the other like the two sides of a coin. If you separated the one from the other God would cease to be God. In Jesus these exist in eternal unity. In the Hebrew liturgy of the synagogue the *Shama* prayer echoes this unity: *"Hear O Israel the Lord your God He is one!"* (see Deut. 6:4).

The picture of the lion in our world has in most cultures and times been seen as a fitting symbol of a king. He is the one who rules. In the movie *The Lion King*, a story for children of all ages, the lion is beautifully and naturally portrayed as the king of all beasts. The Scripture says the lion is the mightiest among the beasts. In the story of *The Lion King* there is also the counterfeit lion—the usurper who prowls about seeking whom he may devour.

The lamb, on the other hand, is a picture of all that is humble and meek. It is of all creatures in need of a shepherd. By its very nature it needs to be cared for, led, and protected. It is a creature that simply responds to the leadership and care of the shepherd. The lamb is a fitting symbol of submission, childlike trust, and responsiveness. It is also a picture of vulnerability, gentleness, and dependence. Jesus was a model of this for us in the way He responded to the Father and His plans for Him. He was obedient as the Father directed Him. Jesus, the Lamb of God, followed all the way to His death, even death on a cross. As "the Lamb" He was also the sacrifice given to redeem the world from sin.

In fallen men and women there is a general revulsion of weakness and an instinctive grasp for power. God in Christ, on the other hand, is deeply in touch with weakness and vulnerability. The radical call of Jesus to us is that we are to lose ourselves in order that we find ourselves. This goes against our fallen natures.

In John 5:19-20, Jesus claimed that of Himself, He had no authority. All authority came from the Father with whom He was one. He did only what He saw the Father doing.

> *Jesus gave them this answer: "I tell you the truth, the Son can do nothing by Himself; He can do only what He sees His Father doing, because whatever the Father does the Son also does. For the Father loves the Son and shows Him all He does. Yes, to your amazement He will show Him even greater things than these."*

In His time on earth all the decisions Jesus makes come from the Father. The Father speaks and Jesus listens and obeys. He does nothing on His own. He is constantly in this amazing position of unpredictable weakness waiting for the next thing the Father would say. Imagine having no plan other than being supernaturally sensitive to the Father and listening for His voice and doing only what is heard. This is not an acceptable picture of leadership and masculine strength in our fallen world. We would never think of running a seminar on leadership based on such a position of vulnerability and weakness. Here is the Son of God with no five-step plan and no evidence of a magnificent and impressive set of goals. He has no plan other than to listen for the Father's voice for the next step.

He who bids us follow Him says, "I have no authority of My own!" Consider this passage from John 5:30:

> *I am able to do nothing from Myself [independently, of My own accord—but only as I am taught by God and as I get His orders]. Even as I hear, I judge [I decide as I am bidden to decide. As the voice comes to Me, so I give a decision], and My judgment is right (just, righteous), because I do not seek or consult My own will [I have no desire to do what is pleasing to Myself, My own aim, My own purpose] but only the will and pleasure of the Father Who sent Me* (AMP).

What kind of King is this? What kind of Kingdom? It is clearly like nothing we have ever known. It is leadership based on weakness. It is an overflowing fullness that comes from emptiness. Paul, who learned this secret from Jesus said, *"I have learned that when I am weak then I am strong"* (see 2 Cor. 12:10). There is no doubt that this kind of leadership would be quite repulsive to the strong of this world. The leaders of this world, if they are worth their salt, need to know where they are going and have a plan based on good principles and sound information. All the Son of God has is the mandate to listen for a voice.

Imagine a political leader of this world trying this on his constituency, "I have no plan other than to be sensitive to what I see and hear from above at the given moment." This is the politics of the Kingdom of Heaven and it is repugnant to the powerful and mighty of this earthly order. God says, *"As the heavens are higher than the earth, so are My ways higher than your ways..."* (Isa. 55:9).

ABRAHAM

There is a wonderful foreshadowing of the leadership style of this coming Kingdom in the life of Abraham in the Old Testament. He is told to leave Ur of the Chaldeans and go where he will be shown. Ur was the place to be if you wanted power and influence. It is considered by scholars to be the cradle of modern civilization and learning. It was where it was all happening in the ancient world.

Abraham hears a voice that says, "Leave! I will take you to another place, a promised land that flows with milk and honey." "What...Where?" he asks. The answer: "I am not telling...Just go...And for today you can head for that mountain in the distance. I'll tell you tomorrow where to go next." The writer to the Hebrews tells us that Abraham went by faith not knowing where he was going. (See Genesis 12.) Can you imagine the insecurity this would provoke in the average man or woman? Abraham would certainly be no candidate for leadership or CEO in the way of thinking of this world.

Abraham's lifestyle is based on pure faith. The lives of Joseph and David ring of the same stuff. All these men are prophetic forerunners of Him who would one day come and bring back to earth the Kingdom of Heaven and its peculiar ways.

Jesus lived His life here on earth as a lamb before the Father. He lived in response to the shepherding voice of His Father. In all purity and humility He was always listening for the Father's will for the next thing He was to say or do. He said, "Without My Father I can do nothing." This was His constant choice. He chose weakness, He chose submission, and He chose emptiness. He would wait for the One who would give Him strength, direction, and fullness. This is the way of relationship and therefore the way of truth. It is the way of love and true joy in relationship and intimacy with the Father. It is the way of a true unfallen man. It is the way to true masculine strength for men and women alike. It is strength born out of weakness, authority born out of submission, the power to initiate born out of the ability to respond. It is the true masculine born out of and one with the true feminine. This is the original plan of the Father for His children. It is the essence of the very life of Heaven.

PERELANDRA STYLE—DE KINE[1]

C.S. Lewis's *Perelandra* tells the story of a man's visit to a young and still innocent new world. The main character of the story, Ransom, finally sees the *unfallen* king and queen of the young planet together. Standing side by side the young king and queen reflect a true likeness of God. He and she together holding hands are a "shadow"—an image of a higher masculine and feminine standing together in perfect marriage. Ransom involuntarily falls at their feet and begs them to take him as their child. He cries out that he has never known a real and true father or mother. He has never before seen a real man or a real woman. All he has ever known in his world are broken images.[2]

A picture of the true masculine and the true feminine is seen in Jesus. Out of an emptiness and a vulnerable childlike trust we see a humble, obedient, and confident response to the Father's voice, followed by the amazing and infinite empowering and authority that is born out of His submission to the Father. In Jesus we see the power to initiate born out of the ability to respond—Lamb and Lion. All is one in Him. In setting this example He says, "Follow Me. I am the true pattern for your life."

In Philippians 2:5-11 Paul encourages us to follow the example set by Jesus:

> *Your attitude should be the same as that of Christ Jesus: who, being in very nature God, did not consider equality with God something to be grasped, but made Himself nothing, taking the very nature of a servant, being made in human likeness. And being found in appearance as a man, He humbled Himself and became obedient to death— even death on a cross! Therefore God exalted Him to the highest place and gave Him the name that is above every name, that at the name of Jesus every knee should bow, in heaven and on earth and under the earth, and every tongue confess that Jesus Christ is Lord, to the glory of God the Father.*

This passage tells us of the great emptying of Jesus before the Father. This was necessary so that the Father could in turn fill Him with heavenly authority and power so that He could bring in the Kingdom of Heaven. Paul says, *"Let this mind be in you that was in Christ"* (see Phil. 2:5 KJV). Jesus is our model. He said, "Follow Me."

SOMETHING TO DO

Prayerfully meditate on Jesus who is both the Lamb of God who was obedient in becoming the sacrifice needed to rescue us and also the risen Lion King to whom all authority in Heaven and earth is given. Out of His humble response to the Father's will is born the true power to initiate and bring the Kingdom of Heaven into this world. In God, these two things,

Lion and Lamb, are one and are inseparable. This is our pattern. This is the Father's original plan for us. We are created in His image!

Since Jesus called you to follow Him, pray through Philippians chapter 2 verses 5-11 asking God to do a work of grace in you in order that you would be the same as Him. Trust Him…He will respond to the sincere prayer of your heart.

ENDNOTES

1. De kine ("the kind") is a Hawaiian colloquial expression that correlates to the Australian "fair dincham" or the American "the real deal."

2. C.S. Lewis, *Perelandra* (New York, NY: Simon & Schuster, 1996).

Chapter Six

THE STORY OF MARY

The angel went to her and said, "Greetings, you who are highly favored! The Lord is with you." Mary was greatly troubled at his words and wondered what kind of greeting this might be. But the angel said to her, "Do not be afraid, Mary, you have found favor with God."

—Luke 1:28-30

"The story," the Bushman prisoner said, "is like the wind. It comes from a far-off place and we feel it."

—Laurens van der Post, *A Story Like the Wind*

A long time ago, God looked down upon the earth He had created and saw the brokenness and sin among the sons and daughters of Adam and Eve. His great heart was pierced with sadness. His beloved children had fallen from what He had originally intended and planned. His image on earth was broken.

He longed to redeem the world, and He knew exactly how He would do it. There was a deep and sacred magic hidden in the heart of God that existed from before the dawn of time that said if an innocent one gave His life in the place of a traitor, then death would start working backward.[1] This magical law of love lived in the heart of God, and so His plan was to send an innocent one, His dear and only Son, into the world to become the means by which death should be destroyed and life come back to His fallen children. This would be His unique and special way to bring His Kingdom—His goodness, His righteousness, and His justice—back to the earth.

Now because His ways are not our ways, and His thoughts not ours, He did not go about it in the way that people would have thought. We would have thought that He would perhaps have sought out some good and just ruler through whom to work, through whom to negotiate. No, He didn't do this. He looked upon the earth and He found a very young and lovely little girl—a young teenager, one who was specially chosen for her childlike faith and ability to respond in obedience. He found whom He was looking for. She was a young girl called Mary who lived with her parents in the town of Nazareth, in the land of Israel.

He sent an emissary of the Kingdom of Heaven, an archangel, to earth as His representative to speak to this little girl, to announce to her the news that she had been very specially chosen to be the means by which Heaven would come back to a lost and fallen world. God did not seek out a great king with an army; He sought out a lamb—a child—a little girl, weak and innocent and quite simple and childlike in her ability to trust. Mary was His chosen way and also His chosen weapon of war against the forces of evil and darkness that had so ravaged and stolen His beautiful world.

MARY'S RESPONSE

On the appointed day, the angel announced: "Blessed are you, Mary, for God has chosen you…You have been especially sought out and God rejoices, for He sees in you the childlike faith and obedience necessary to restore His goodness, holiness, and His Kingdom to the earth." And so the angel told her that she would bear in her womb the very life of Heaven itself. The great King of kings, the very Son of God, Light of light, Truth of truth, would come and, as a seed, be put into her womb. In time, she would give birth to the One who is the Son of the Most High, Emmanuel—God with us. (See Luke 1:26-33.)

Now she understood that this would mean some great act of incredible intimacy between her and God. She questioned God and said, "I am just a little girl, and I am a virgin. How will this thing happen?" The angel told her that the very breath of God, the Spirit of the most High God, would come upon her, and she would conceive and bear a child, and His name was to be Jesus, the Son of the Most High. Her response is no doubt what God, in His wonderful foresight, had already foreseen, *"Be it unto me according to your word, for I am the handmaiden of the Lord"* (see Luke 1:38).

And so this little girl with childlike trust says "yes" to the eternal Father. She does not resort to rationalizations about whether or not she is doing the right thing. She knows this is God! After all, she is doing something quite contrary to the rules of her culture. Becoming pregnant before the marital consummation of her engagement to Joseph, her fiancée, would certainly be frowned upon most severely. She was, after all, in the eyes of her community a good girl...a righteous girl. It is important here to observe that she does not tell the angel that she should first go and speak to her father and her mother to discuss it with them or to ask their permission. Nor does she consult Joseph, the one to whom she is betrothed. She simply knows who it is who is visiting her, and she is full of confident trust.

Mary is a wonderful child with great innocence and a capacity to respond to God in intimate trust. Furthermore, God does not go to her parents; God does not consult with Joseph or ask his permission. God does not consult with the current religious order. Nor does He consult with the rulers of the region. Not very diplomatic! No, He finds a child, an innocent little girl, who in the rank of authority among men is the least. She is the lowest rung on the ladder of power and authority. In her society she had no voice, no vote. She did not even belong to herself—she belonged to her father. And it was for her father to one day give her away to another man, in this case the man Joseph to whom she had been betrothed. She had no choice—or did she?

Within her culture, as a young girl, Mary understood that she did not belong to herself and that she would always, as a symbol of all that is creaturely, belong to someone else. In meeting God, she knew instinctively that she was before the One who was the Creator of all things, and that this was the One to whom we all ultimately belong. It was not a decision of rational thought; it was an instinctive, intuitive decision—she knew who this was and so she knew who she was and what to do. She knew with all her heart to say, "Yes…I am Your child; I am Your creature; I am Yours."

It is probable that Mary tried to explain to her parents what had happened. I can imagine the struggle. I can see her astonished father thinking that she had an incredible and frightening imagination. I can imagine her mother being worried about the emotional stability and sanity of what, up until now, had been a perfectly wonderful child. I can imagine her shock and the fear that perhaps it just might actually be true, and what would it all mean? The reaction of her family would no doubt have been similar to that of Lucy Pevensey's brothers and sister in *The Lion, the Witch and the Wardrobe* when she claimed to have found a whole new world inside a wardrobe!

After a while, of course, the young Mary would begin to show and then would come the awful difficulty of dealing with the response of the religious community and neighborhood in which her family lived. They were righteous and good people and no doubt were a prominent family in the local synagogue. As things progressed there was no doubt some discussion about the matter by the local Pharisees and priests and leaders of the religious community. And then there was the gossip among the townsfolk. I can imagine the strange expressions on the faces of the men as they contemplated the peculiar news. I imagine that many of them simply put it up to a child who had been taken advantage of or was experiencing some kind of lunacy. But then there she was, pregnant, and for all the world to see. No doubt many were greatly shocked and appalled at the ridiculous story that this was God's doing. Others, no doubt, merely laughed.

GOD'S CALL TO JOSEPH

Now Joseph, we are told, was a good man, and after thought and discussion with counselors, friends, and family, he decided to "put her away"—that is, to divorce her quietly so as not to make a fuss of it and further hurt and injure the girl (see Matt. 1:19). In this remarkable story, it is not known how many people may have taken the story seriously or not. It is possible her mother did, and in her heart with great fear and apprehension, anticipated the unfolding of a great and wonderful mystery.

The story goes on…God spoke to Joseph in a dream to tell him, "It is just as Mary has said." God then required Joseph to take Mary to be his wife, to look after her, and to take care of the child (see Matt. 1:18-24). Here we have a godly and good young man having to fly in the face of public convention and obey God. "What! Has Joseph now joined this young girl in her madness?" Things are not made easy by God. Obedience to Jesus often has a sense of awkwardness and discomfort about it.

The time comes for a census to be taken and everyone is to return to the towns of their birth. Joseph and Mary go to Bethlehem. It is while they are there that her time to give birth comes, and so in a strange stable far away from the familiar comforts of home, the eternal Light of Heaven comes into a dark world. Goodness incarnate takes His first gulp of created air. In and through Mary the eternal Creator comes as a man into His creation… child is born. His name is Emmanuel—God with us. (See Luke 2:1-7.)

No doubt Mary is full of awe and joy and longs to return home to the safe security of her home where she can begin to take care of the child, but it is not to be so. There is more difficulty…King Herod hears of the child born to be king and in his insane jealousy begins to seek for the babe in order to kill Him. Again in a dream, God speaks to Joseph and tells him they are to go to Egypt. They flee with very little notice and for two years are refugees in a foreign land, far away from family and friends. (See Matthew 2.)

Here are two people, Joseph and Mary, who understand their nature as creatures. They understand their lives are not their own, and as such they are caught up in something higher and greater and bigger than they can imagine. The wind and breath of Heaven comes sweeping down to earth and carries them away into an unpredictable story with the intent to change the world forever.

God's ways are higher than our ways and certainly not what we would have chosen had it been in our hands to choose. If it was our calling to bring about the Kingdom of God on earth, no doubt we would have called upon some strong, stout men (or angels) to do the job. This is not God's way. He found Himself a little girl, young and innocent and weak, someone whose simple understanding of authority was that her work in life was to respond and to obey. This is the true work of submission. This is the secret of how the mystery and wisdom of Heaven works. This is God's way to bring the essential power of life and His eternal Kingdom back to the world. This was God's way to confront evil, to destroy the power of death, and to crush the very power of hell itself. All God needed was a little girl who understood who He was and who understood who she was. This flies in the face of how fallen men think. None of the "important" people are consulted. No ceremony and no extraordinary measures—a mere girl gives birth to a child in a stable.

Who is Mary? What is Mary? What does she represent? What does she symbolize for us? She is perhaps a symbol of everything that is creaturely, of everything that is responsive and of all that lives in submission to the great heart of the Creator. God speaks and she listens with childlike trust. God takes action and she responds with devoted obedience. And so salvation comes into the world.

In the end, Joseph follows Mary's example. He too had to learn to listen and respond and obey. It was not his to decide. It was not his to exercise absolute leadership. He had to in turn follow the One who had spoken to the young girl to whom he was betrothed. It is stunning and mind-blowing to think of what this story tells us about women—and in this case a mere young girl. The story teaches us that God takes a little girl and raises her up into a place of such incredible honor, a place of such influence and power. For this reason, some have unfortunately and mistakenly made her into a god. Nonetheless, we are all beholden to this little girl whom we know as Mary. She truly is our mother in teaching us the ways of God; in teaching us the way of submission, the way of trust, the way of the heart, the way of childlike response to the Creator. Her understanding of who she is as a creature before her Creator is something we must all learn from her if we are going to make it out of this world and into the Kingdom that her obedience brought to us.

WHAT OF TODAY?

How does the Kingdom of Heaven come to our world today—in our day and age, to our town, to our city, and in our families? The ways of God have not changed; they are still the same. The Creator still looks down from Heaven, and He looks for the heart attitude of Mary in each one of His children—the heart of the creature who understands that it is not his or her place to be in control, to be in charge. It is his place to respond, to hear, to listen, and to follow and obey the rule of Love as it comes to us in the person of God the Father, Son, and Holy Spirit. It is out of this kind of obedient response to Jesus that the eternal goodness of Heaven still comes to the world today—real goodness, the kind that comes from knowing the living presence and power of God and not simply the rules He sends. True eternal love and power always come to us in this way. The way it was with Mary is the way it is for us today…it is the way of Heaven.

THE WEDDING

There is another wonderful story about Mary that tells us more of who this remarkable person was. It happens 30 years later. It is God's appointed time for the ministry of Jesus to be released. It is time for the presence and energy of the Kingdom of Heaven to become manifest on earth. It all happens at a wedding feast in Cana of Galilee. Here again, and not by chance, Mary is at the center of the story (see John 2).

The time has come for the High King of Heaven to begin His work, and Mary is there waiting and ready for it. She is involved with the catering at the wedding. Jesus and the disciples arrive at the wedding and we are told that the wine runs out.[2] There is a familiar quickening in Mary's intuitive heart. An idea formulates in her imagination—there is an excitement in her breast. She sees her son, Jesus, and somehow she who is God's chosen creature knows it is time. And so she goes to Him, looks piercingly into His eyes, and says, "The wine has run out." She instinctively knew the time had come for Him to reveal who He was, and the present task at hand was that wine was needed! She knew that Jesus could and somehow would save the day. She knew it was time for His ministry to begin.

Jesus says to her—and I imagine with a smile—"Why do you ask Me, woman? Surely you know it is not My time." I don't believe Jesus is lying here. He too knows it's time. He is just marveling in a peculiarly Jewish way at the fact that she knows. He is astounded that this incredibly wonderful woman knows that it is time. I can only imagine the excitement in her voice, the joy in her laughter, and the light shining in her eyes when she gives the command to the servants. Ignoring what He said and pointing to Jesus, she says to the servants, "Do whatever He tells you." By this beautiful command, which came from Mary, the manifestation of His kingly power and authority is released and made known. Water is changed into wine! For the Hebrew people, wine is a high symbol of life and friendship and love and of all that is good and holy in family, in community, and in marriage.[3] There is a beautiful picture here of the relationship God desires between Himself and His creatures. It is perhaps no mistake that this occurs at a marriage celebration. At the wedding there is also a marvelous indication of the marriage that exists between the intent of God and the intuitive trust and response of Mary, God's creature, to collaborate with the Father in a further bringing of the Kingdom of Heaven to earth.

A MARRIAGE FEAST

All of God's children are on a journey headed for a great marriage feast when we will one day drink the new wine with Jesus in Heaven. I would not be the least surprised if Mary plays a significant role at that occasion. She understands what it means to be a creature and she knows and loves God as her Father. She was created with a capacity to respond, to imagine, to see, to know, to hear, to perceive, to listen, and to obey.

It is when these feminine attributes of life are restored in each of us that we are able to fully come alive and become the true initiators and leaders that God would have us be. It is in this way that the life and good leadership of Heaven comes back to this planet we call Earth. It is in this way that the powers of darkness are defeated. It is in this way that death is destroyed.

It is in this way that the family life of the Kingdom of Heaven is resurrected in us and re-established for all eternity. The Kingdom is restored not because of the lofty thoughts and prowess of the "adult" men in our midst but because of the simplicity of the child within each of us. This includes men, women, and the children in our communities. It is the ability of the true childlike creature within each of us, to know, love, and trust the Creator that brings Heaven into our hearts. We are told in Scripture that we would be led by a child…perhaps this includes the child within? It is thus that we have life and are rescued from an eternal and fiery death.

It Is the Same Now

For you and me, the same Holy Spirit does the same work of mysterious and awesome magic He did 2,000 years ago in the womb of Mary. Like Mary, we too must respond. It is imperative! We must say "yes" to Him who is the High King so that the advent of Christmas would live every day within us. With true joy our hearts sing, "Yes Lord, yes Lord, yes, yes Lord!" That Christ should come again in your heart and in my heart and in all the hearts of all men and women who are willing (whether they know it or not) to take their lead from Mary and follow in the pattern she set for us. She is a mother, a teacher, and an influential leader to the Church.[4] She, above all, has taught us how to respond, trust, obey, and follow Jesus. This is the way of the Kingdom. There is no other way.

It is when men and women forget her example and choose to become controlling, domineering, and manipulative that the life of Heaven is lost. It is in this way we destroy the things that we have built up—whether it be our family or the local church or the ministry that God has given us. At some point we fancy that we know, that we have learnt, and so we grasp at control as we reach out for the tree of the knowledge of good and evil (mere technical knowledge based on rational dogma and formulae—"the facts") as the determining basis and source of life, identity, and decision making. Like the "enlightened" Voltaire of the 19th century, we falsely imagine we have "come of age."

In the face of such grown-up, "enlightened" knowledge Jesus says, *"Truly, truly I tell you, unless you change and become like little children, you shall not inherit the kingdom of heaven"* (see Matt. 18:3).

SOMETHING TO DO

Prayerfully consider what you can learn from Mary's childlike response and obedience to the Father. Consider how such obedience and submission bring about the advent of His presence on earth. Humbly offer yourself in faith to such obedience in order that the living presence of God and His Kingdom may become incarnate in you and therefore in your world.

ENDNOTES

1. The concept of "the deep magic" is taken from C.S. Lewis's *The Lion, the Witch and the Wardrobe*. It represents God's law and ways.

2. For wine to run out at a Hebrew wedding is a particularly serious and embarrassing event for the host. This is because, for the Hebrew people, wine is a significant symbol of life, relationship, covenant, and marriage. It is in the context of this culture that Jesus seals the new covenant by sharing bread and wine with the disciples.

3. Wine is an integral part of the Hebrew wedding ceremony. At one point the in the marriage ceremony the groom and bride drink a glass of wine together, and then the glass is broken underfoot to symbolize the sealing of the covenant of marriage.

4. I do not mean this in a way that elevates Mary into position where she is worshiped. The true Mary would be horrified at such an awful mistake. She is a mere creature whose great work is to point us to Jesus and teach us how to trust and obey His will.

Chapter Seven

THE TWO TREES

Religion is not a matter of learning how to think about God,
but of actually encountering Him.

—Brennan Manning, *Lion and Lamb*

And the Lord God made all kinds of trees grow out of the
ground—trees that were pleasing to the eye and good for food.
In the middle of the garden were the tree of life and the tree
of the knowledge of good and evil.

—Genesis 2:9

The tongue that brings healing is a tree of life, but a deceitful
tongue crushes the spirit.

—Proverbs 15:4

THE two trees in the center of the Garden of Eden, among other things, speak to us of opposites, or polarity. There is the tree of life and the tree of the knowledge of good and evil. What they represent lies at the heart of human life—indeed, the very heart and center of all things! Their meaning is indispensable and inseparable, and through the use of symbolic pictures and parables, God is able to communicate to us multiple things on different levels that He truly wants us to understand. Therefore, we need to understand how the trees symbolize relationship, especially the polar differences between the masculine and the feminine. We especially need to understand how we have gotten it wrong by "eating" from the tree of knowledge instead of the tree of life.

THE TREE OF LIFE

The *tree of life* is essentially a symbol of organic relationship. Words and concepts in the Hebrew language lean heavily toward the poetic and pictorial. The word for *life* in Hebrew conjures up pictures of relationship, integration, peace, and unity. If we are friends and are one in love and purpose, we have unity. We have "life"! If we are enemies we are apart and death and separation reign. In Hebrew thinking separation, divorce, disintegration, and division are the opposites of life and therefore the enemies of Heaven. These things are the elements of death and their ultimate home is hell. Life and death are like marriage and divorce. God is the God of marriage and His desire is to live in a covenant union with His children based on faith, hope, and love. He wants more than anything else to be one with the children He created. The Scriptures tell us that He sees Himself both as a Parent with children and as a Husband with His Bride. In John chapter 17 Jesus, in preparation for His death, prays for this union life. At the beginning of the prayer He says, *"Now this is eternal life: that they may know You, the only true God, and Jesus Christ, whom You have sent"* (John 17:3-5). Further along in the chapter He prays, *"Father, as You and I are one may they be one..."* (see John 17:21). This is a prayer for life!

Before the Fall Adam and Eve together symbolized a tree of life inasmuch as they drew life and identity from their relationship and intimacy with the Father. They were loved and led by the Father. Relationship with the Father was their very source of life and the root from which they drew their identity. Paul, expressing the essence of salvation, once said, *"For me to live is Christ"* (see Phil. 1:21). The tree of life represents a way "of being" in which new and fresh life and relationship is constantly being born and nurtured through intimacy with and immediate trust in God. It represents an essential way of being that gives and nourishes the very life of Heaven Himself.

In this sense, His giving of life to us has a great maternal quality. It is normally a mother who brings new life into the world and is able to nurse and nurture that life so that it can grow to its full potential. Our primary work is to respond to His gift of life to us. Once we have been nourished and empowered by the Lord, we are then sent out to go and do the works He has prepared for us to do.

The Tree of Knowledge

The tree of knowledge of good and evil, on the other hand, symbolizes the law and as such includes the knowledge of structure and order. To be a tree of knowledge of good and evil is simply to receive your identity from the mere knowledge about God and His ways. We speak here of not just the moral law but the laws that govern all things—from raising children to running a business, from medical science to physics. The law, or structure and order, procedure and rules, by itself does not have or give life; it provides containment and protection for it. God forbids that we "eat" from this tree of knowledge. We are told it will poison and kill us. On a purely physical level, it is obvious that we receive life from what we eat. From ancient times people have believed that you become what you eat. God's instruction is that we do not seek life and nourishment from the tree of knowledge, that is, the law—the mere knowledge of things.

Jesus' use of the illustration of wine and wineskins helps us to understand this. Wine in the Hebrew culture is a symbol of life and, therefore, relationship. In the Hebrew culture, when people gather together as family and friends they break bread and drink wine. If they were to also eat the wineskin it would certainly do them harm. The wineskin is nonetheless a cardinal necessity for the containment and protection of the wine! Without it the wine would be lost. It is the bread and wine that give us life and not the means of their delivery. However, this symbolic picture shows us that the very things that give us life would be lost without the necessary structure for their containment and successful delivery. Structure and law are given to us as an essential service to contain and protect life. We need the rules and the order they provide.

The law is also there to tell us when things go wrong. It draws the lines that are not to be crossed and tells us what sin is. The law teaches us that the life God gives us and the life we are thereby able to give each other will be damaged and lost if we do not listen to it, respect its boundaries, and follow its directives. It provides protection for life and relationship. In and of itself the law does not bring or give life. Life and relationship emanate from God and are received and shared by us.

THE TWO TREES TOGETHER

On another level, perhaps the tree of life speaks more about being and the tree of knowledge more about doing. The two go together and are inseparable and essential. They grow at the center of the Garden of Life and are rightly alongside each other. Knowledge protects life but does not give it. In fact, we are told that if we go to it seeking life we will lose the life we have and die. We are categorically told not to eat from the tree of knowledge of good and evil! What the tree of knowledge represents is predominantly masculine in character. It empowers and provides the necessary structure, boundary lines, protection, order, guidelines, and direction. Grasping for the fruit of this tree as a source of life represents a rejection of the feminine principle in life—that is, the call on our lives to first respond to the leadership of God before we take action or initiate anything ourselves. With the great gift of God's presence, all we can do is respond…to eat and drink and be nourished by it. Thus, as we listen for Him, we are empowered to live and take action in His name.

So we have wine and we have wineskins, life and structure. Both are central to our existence. They exist in a divinely ordained marriage, vastly different and at the same time strangely and inseparably one!

If we look at the picture provided by the different physiologies of a man and a woman, we see the same theme. On a purely physiological and regenerative level the woman, who represents the creature, responds to the man, who represents the Creator, by offering him the empty space that only he can fill. She conceives, gives birth, and, through her God-ordained nurturing powers, families and communities are brought into being. The man is called upon to plant the seed and provide the covenantal covering and loving protection that would contain and protect the gift of nurturing life and family relationships that flow from the woman. Human coitus, in its redeemed form, is a symbolic representation of the transcendent and holy life-giving intimacy between the Creator and His creatures.

WHEN THERE IS NO DEMOCRACY...

When God wants to invade earth with the life of Heaven, He goes first to Mary. She is the means by which Immanuel comes to earth. Then God goes to Joseph when He wants protection and covering for this life. Joseph is to take Mary as his wife. He is to love, protect, and provide for her and the life that God would bring into the world through her obedience. God tells Joseph in a dream to take Mary and go to Egypt in order to get the mother and child to safety. It is his appointed work, and any other course he might take would be disobedience. There is no democracy about these different roles.

The Kingdom of God is neither a democracy nor a dictatorship. God is not a tyrannical ruler who would force obedience or demand that we be as slaves. He gave us a free will in the hope that we would freely choose to obey the truth. We do not get to decide who gives birth and has the greatest capacity and responsibility in nurturing or who plants the seed of life and gets the bulk of the servant work of provision and direction. There is an inherent common sense and natural logic contained within our gender that we are to respond to and obey if we are to be true men and women. C.S. Lewis, in his book *The Hideous Strength*, suggests that the Church is not some neutral or democratic vacuum in which sense and sexuality simply disappear.[1] There is order in life, such as gravity, that God has ordained and that we cannot change, and our contrary opinions will not profit us. Many things are simply the way they are and we are to respond. It is a matter of obedience and good sense!

This principle of initiating and responding applies in many ways to the material world about us. An artist understands there is no democracy about the qualities and nature of light and color. He does not decide what yellow is nor does he change the dynamics of light and shadows. He learns to respond to what "is" if he is ever going to become a true artist. The same is true of music, mathematics, and physics. In all things pertaining to life someone has taken initiative and therefore another must respond. It makes for relationship and therefore truth.[2] It is the feminine aspect of life within each of us that gives us the ability to respond to what is, and thereby we are enabled to grow and learn—to become.

SPEAKING AND LISTENING

This principle can also be illustrated by the idea of speaking and listening. Communication exists only if someone says something and someone else listens. Speaking by itself does not give life or relationship. It is the response of listening to what is spoken that does it. In our illustration of speaking and listening, it is not, perhaps, merely coincidental that the physical shape of the tongue is, symbolically, masculine and the ear feminine. It is even more so with the genitalia. One shape is a void or emptiness and the other shape is that which can perfectly fill the emptiness. There is no notion of superiority and inferiority in this. It gives a clear message about perfect equality in a sublime and life-giving unity and marriage. The one needs the other equally. On their own they are incomplete, reflecting more of a caricature of their Creator, needing the other to properly reflect the character of the One who created them.

I can say to my child, "I love you." However, it is the child's response that determines whether what I say becomes a matter of life and joy and thereby the existence and furtherance of relationship. In the same way God takes the initiative and says to His sons and daughters, "I love you." It is our acceptance and response that determine whether life and relationship occur. When I respond and believe, then and only then is the truth of it established within me. The connection is made and the circle is complete. If I choose unbelief then I remain in a state of separation and therefore death. That is, I am cut off.

In the letter to the Hebrews chapters 3 and 4 we are told how an entire generation of the children of Israel missed the opportunity to enter the Promised Land and lost the "rest" that God would have given them.

> *So, as the Holy Spirit says: Today, if you hear His voice, do not harden your hearts as you did in the rebellion, during the time of testing in the desert, where your fathers tested and tried Me and for forty years saw what I did. That is why I was angry with that generation, and I said, "Their hearts are always going astray, and they have not known My ways." So I declared on oath in My anger, "They shall never enter My rest." See to it, brothers, that none of you has a sinful, unbelieving heart that turns away from the living God. But encourage one another daily, as long as it is called Today, so that none of you may be hardened by sin's deceitfulness. We have come to share in Christ if we hold firmly till the end the confidence we had at first. As has just been said: "Today, if you hear His voice, do not harden your hearts as you did in the rebellion"* (Hebrews 3:7-15).

If we miss listening, we miss it all! The meaning of God's Word to us in the picture of the tree of life is about our ability to listen for and respond to the initiative of another (especially in regard to God) and so receive life within us. The tree of knowledge can symbolize our responsibility to provide structure and protection for that life. What these two trees together represent lives eternally in God, side by side, perhaps the one within the other. As individuals, all men and women have the ability to initiate and respond. However, men, in certain limited and prescribed circumstances, are to provide and demonstrate leadership in the art of initiative, and women, in certain limited and prescribed circumstances, are to be the representation of the peculiar and beautiful art of response. Nowhere is this more poignantly played out than upon the stage of our human sexuality where, during coitus, a poetic drama is performed, representing and symbolizing a higher and transcendent reality that exists in the great dance between Heaven and creation. It speaks to us of great and holy things…Let us keep it holy!

The one without the other is inevitable death. It is what makes marriage possible on every level of life. It is what makes family. Only as the two polar forces of masculine and feminine engage in a spiritual marriage do we come to breathe the very life-giving air of Heaven Himself.

SOMETHING TO DO

Take time to ask God to show you how you are doing on your journey to becoming a *tree of life*. That is, seek to become someone who is learning to live your life out of the secure knowledge of being the Father's child—rooted and established in love—and not someone who is still striving to find significance and identity out of performance based on mere knowledge. Ask Him to rescue you with His love so that you would be able to measure all the height and width and depth of His love—to know this love that cannot be known by mere human intelligence and so be filled with all the fullness of God.

ENDNOTES

1. C.S. Lewis, *That Hideous Strength* (New York, NY: Simon & Schuster, 1965) 315.

2. Truth is always about relationship. Truth does not exist without contrast and connection to something or someone else.

Chapter Eight

LOVE—THE SOURCE OF TRUE IDENTITY

L'amour de Dieu est folie[1]

—From the French Easter liturgy

*"What makes the temptation of power so seemingly irresistible?
Maybe it is that power offers an easy substitute for the hard
task of love. It seems easier to be God than to love God, easier
to control people than to love people, easier to own life than to
love life. Jesus asks, 'Do you love me?' We ask, 'Can we sit at
your right hand and your left hand in your Kingdom?' (Matthew
20:21). Ever since the snake said, 'The day you eat of this tree
your eyes will be open and you will be like gods, knowing good
from evil' (Genesis 3:5), we have been tempted to replace love
with power. Jesus lived that temptation in the most agonizing
way from the desert to the cross. The long painful history of the
Church is the history of people ever and again tempted to choose
power over love, control over the cross, being a leader over being
led. Those who resisted this temptation to the end and
thereby give us hope are the true saints.*

*"One thing is clear to me: the temptation of power is greatest
when intimacy is a threat. Much Christian leadership is exercised
by people who do not know how to develop healthy, intimate
relationships and have opted for power and control instead. Many
Christian empire-builders have been people unable to
give and receive love."*

—Henri J.M. Nouwen[2]

THE two trees in the Scriptures are essential to the understanding of
life. The Bible begins with the two trees in the Garden of Eden, and
as it ends in the last chapter of the Book of Revelation, there is a
reference to the tree of life growing in Heaven.

> *...down the middle of the great street of the city. On each
> side of the river stood the tree of life, bearing twelve crops
> of fruit, yielding its fruit every month. And the leaves of the
> tree are for the healing of the nations. No longer will there
> be any curse. The throne of God and of the Lamb will be
> in the city, and His servants will serve Him* (Revelation
> 22:2-3).

What happened to the other tree? It is, in a way, mentioned in this verse:
"No longer will there be any curse." In his letter to the Galatians, Paul
refers to the law as a curse (see Gal. 3:10,13). The law, as Jesus promised,
has become fulfilled and is mysteriously and wonderfully taken up into
the tree of life. With the work of redemption complete He now lives in His
people and the law is written on their hearts and as such is fulfilled. Jesus
said He had not come to do away with the law but to fulfill it. He not only
fulfills the law by dying in our place, thereby satisfying the law's demands
by taking our sin upon Himself and paying for it, but He also fulfills the law
by taking us out from under it and placing us "under" the intimate direction of the Holy Spirit. The Spirit then reveals and writes the ways of God

and the laws of God's love on our hearts. When we are redeemed we are taken out from living under the law that condemns us and brought into personal relationship with God. This is the very thing we are saved for, that we would be one with the Father. This signifies a shift from the Old Covenant to the New. This is the Good News!

When there is intimacy with God, recognition of the Father's love, and obedience to what He says, there is no more need to be "under the law." The law is not done away with but fulfilled! The law is taken up into a level of holiness and righteousness that transcends the simplistic and prosaic righteousness of the law. The Pharisees drew their identity from knowledge—their knowledge and practice of the law. Jesus drew His identity from relationship, His relationship with the Father. The difference is enormous—as high as the heavens are above the earth! Jesus demonstrated to us that real relationship with the Father is the source of all true holiness and righteousness.

In John chapter 5 Jesus said; *"I do only what I see the Father doing."* He went on to say, *"I have no authority of My own. As I hear I judge and My judgment is right because I seek not My own will but the will of Him who sent Me"* (see John 5:19,30). He lived and drew His identity out of looking at and listening to the Father. He did not do His own thing but only what the Father showed Him. All He said and did came from a secure and splendid intimacy with the Father. This is essentially who He is. He does not exist apart from being one with the Father. He called His disciples to follow Him! They are to live in the same way! This represents a major shift in the way we think…from the law to the Spirit!

A Tree—A Symbol of Identity

Throughout the Bible trees are used as symbols for humans and our human identities. We are told to be "trees of righteousness" planted by God. In Psalm 1 there is a beautiful and poetic reference to being like a tree.

Blessed is the man who does not walk in the counsel of
the wicked or stand in the way of sinners or sit in the seat

of mockers. But his delight is in the law of the Lord, and
on His law he meditates day and night. He is like a tree
planted by streams of water, which yields its fruit in season
and whose leaf does not wither. Whatever he does prospers
(Psalm 1:1-3).

People who do not trust God are like bushes growing in the desert, but
those who put their trust in God are like trees continually drinking in the
deep water of life that comes from friendship with God. Their leaves never
fade and they always bear fruit.

This is what the Lord says: "Cursed is the one who trusts
in man, who depends on flesh for his strength and whose
heart turns away from the Lord. He will be like a bush in
the wastelands; he will not see prosperity when it comes.
He will dwell in the parched places of the desert, in a salt
land where no one lives. But blessed is the man who trusts
in the Lord, whose confidence is in Him. He will be like
a tree planted by the water that sends out its roots by the
stream. It does not fear when heat comes; its leaves are
always green. It has no worries in a year of drought and
never fails to bear fruit" (Jeremiah 17:5-8).

In the last chapter of Revelation there is a marvelous picture of God the
Father and Jesus the Lamb on the throne. From the throne flows a river of
life—the very life of God Himself flowing to the city. The river is a picture
of the Spirit, the very life of God, flowing from the Father and the Son, giving life to Heaven. The throne is the center of authority and life for the Holy
Trinity. The tree of life is growing on both sides of the river. What do these
things represent? We know the Lamb is Jesus and the River represents the
Spirit and life of God. The tree of life, therefore, is us, the saints, the Bride
of Christ, receiving life from the presence of God. The great family of saints
is the tree of life. The saints have become what they have eaten! They have
eaten the bread and wine offered by Jesus and they have become a tree of
life, a symbol of how things are to be in the end (or perhaps the beginning).

These beautiful, poetic pictures help us imagine what the culmination of God's great plan of redemption will look like.

Jesus, who received His identity from intimacy with the Father, is our pattern and example. He said, "Follow Me." We are to be re-made in His image! Like Jesus we are to become a tree of life, living our life and receiving our identity from the eternal Father.

LIFE AND DEATH

The Hebrew language is similar to the Chinese language in its way of thinking. "Words" are drawn rather than written. It is a poetic language in which the predominant way to communicate is with pictures, symbols, and stories. The Greek language leans more to a left-brained logical and rational way of thinking. Both patterns of thought are valid and even essential, however the Bible is written in the context of and by a people and culture that is Hebrew, and therefore its way of thinking and communication is predominantly picture and story oriented. The question, "Have you got the picture?" is appropriate to ask in attempting to understand the meaning of a Hebrew word.

As I mentioned earlier, the word for *life* in Hebrew is a word that conveys a picture of relationship, family, and friendship. The word *death* communicates a picture of separation which includes the "death" of relationships. For instance, the Hebrew people did not eat or have fellowship with the Samaritans. They would say that the Samaritans were dead. By this they meant they were separated from them, did not have fellowship with them, and therefore, did not eat with them, as meals were inseparable from "life" and relationship. Even to this day in some strict orthodox Jewish families, if a daughter marries a gentile, the family declares their daughter to be dead.

I knew a Jewish woman who became a Christian, resulting in her family declaring her dead. They said the prayers for the dead for her—what the Hebrew people call *Kaddish*. When she would see her family in the city, they would walk past her, ignoring her attempts to speak with them. Her family had even performed a special ceremony in which they had symbolically buried her. When the Hebrew people used the word *death,* they understood it to mean separation and the end of relationship. The effect of physical death is, after all, severe separation—the person is gone and will not return!

When Scripture tells us, *"The soul that sins will die"* (see Ezek. 18:4), it makes a lot of sense if you think in the Hebrew way that sin causes the breakdown of relationship and therefore brings about separation. People are torn apart from God and each other by sin. Trust is crushed and stripped away. The ingredients of relationship, truth, and life are destroyed and we are left with brokenness, division, and separation. The soul that sins will die! God told Adam and Eve that they would die if they ate from the tree of the knowledge of good and evil. When they disobeyed, they did die. Terrible separation came upon them and they suddenly found themselves in a state of death, separated from God and the paradise garden that was their home.

PIRATES

In the movie *Pirates of the Caribbean,* the pirates are under a curse for stealing some gold coins and have been turned into the "undead"— people who have no life, but they still move about as if alive; their souls are stuck in limbo. (In the Caribbean they call such creatures Zombies.) They continue to exist in a way that is empty and void of life, yet they cannot be killed or destroyed. They are not able to taste food or experience joy or happiness. To love is impossible. They have no connection, no relationship. They have no ability to feel anything. All they are aware of is their intolerable and dreary emptiness. These scenes paint a good picture of what death is like. Death is not an "end" but a state of horrific separation and "lifeless" existence.

God wants us to be alive! That means that we are to have our roots and identity in relationship and love. This is a biblical picture of what life is. Where our roots go down determines who we are. Are our roots receiving poison from the lies of the enemy that would kill us, or are we receiving life from the truth of God's Word revealed to us and His love poured out? Jesus wants us to be a tree of life with our roots secure in the Father heart of God.

When I think of the word *father*, I have a picture of God loving me and embracing me. My personal experience of God has made me into a tree of life. It is now part of who I am. I am loved by God; this is a part of my essential core identity. I am loved—that's the heart of who I am. I belong to Somebody. I don't belong to myself; I belong to God. I belong to my Father, and He has given Himself to me forever. This, *more than anything,* changes my behavior and enables me to live in obedience to love. It is what enables me to love others. It enables me to be "good." His Spirit living within is like a spring of living water bubbling up inside that enables me to know I am immensely loved by God...embraced by His grace, His forgiveness, His goodness, and His eternal life-giving presence. Rules do not accomplish this.

Who Is God to You?

Graham Cooke encourages us to ask ourselves, "What is the most unique way in which God reveals Himself to me?" For Graham, God has revealed His kindness. It is for this reason that Graham can joyfully say, "God is the kindest person I know." This revelation from the Holy Spirit to him is what makes Graham Cooke who he is and does much to establish his identity. He knows who he is in relation to God's kindness. It is not being a famous Bible teacher or a global prophetic figure that counts. That is just peripheral; knowing God firsthand is what gives a person their true identity.

For me, God has revealed His love. I know that I am loved by God. This fills me with childlike trust and the joyful ability to love Him back. For my wife, Clare, God has revealed Himself as her Provider. This enables her to trust God to take care of her every need and those of her family. The way God reveals Himself to us shapes who we become. Each of us is unique to God and He has a unique way in which He has chosen to reveal Himself to us.

The fruit our lives bear comes from what we are rooted in. The flow of life is from the roots upwards to the fruit and not the other way. Life is first about receiving and "being" and second about doing and giving. You cannot give what you have not received…and you cannot receive life only from what you do. If I am a medical doctor that is not who I am, it is what I do. I practice medicine. If I am loved and valued by God then that is who I am. I am loved. I am precious. He is the great "I Am" who out of His great love tells me who I am.

A small boy who is the grandson of a dear friend eagerly told her that he had scored a goal in a soccer game. She remarked how glad she was and pointed out that she loved him regardless of whether he scored a goal or not. He ran off giggling at the thought!

Once "being" is in its proper place, then what we do has greater power and value. Brennan Manning tells a story of a dear old friend of his who was found walking down a country road in Ireland with tears streaming down his face. When asked why he was weeping, he simply answered, "The Father is very fond of me…the Father is very fond of me." May we all, in time, come to see this and so be healed.

A True Name

Isaiah 43:1 says, *"…Fear not, for I have redeemed you; I have sum-moned you by name."* God has a name for you, and He is trying to tell you what your name is—He's trying to tell you who you are. In this passage He says, *"I have summoned you by name…"* followed by, *"You are Mine."* This is the most significant part of your name—that you belong to Him… in a unique way. And then there is a lot more that would take the rest of your life for Him to tell, but it begins with, "Fear not, you are Mine." It is probable that God has a long name for each one of us since there is a lot to tell about each of us.

Some years ago I was at a Hawaiian first birthday celebration on the Big Island of Hawaii. The name given to the child was long enough to take up two lines of writing. Her name told a story of the circumstances of her birth and something of the context of her life. After hearing her very long name we were told to "call her Nunu for short." Her full name was virtually a story telling us who she was. Western people would be enriched if they would seek to understand this way of thinking. In many cultures, it is unthinkable to name a child until it is born and their family has met them and know who they are.

God will take the rest of your life to tell you who you are. It takes time to find out what your true name is. God is the "Mother and Father" who also created you and knit you together in your mother's womb, and He desires to be the One to tell you your name and give you your true identity. From your birth, He has had a name for you—a secret name, known only to Him. Your true identity and destiny can only come from Him. Your true name is a predestined story and the eternal Father alone can tell that story—if you let Him. No one else can tell you your real name! All else is illusion and shadow.

When He creates us, He knows "who" He is creating. Only as our roots grow down in intimacy with God and we come to know this love and learn to hear His voice do we begin to receive revelations of who He is and who we truly are. Over the years as we grow in obedience to the leading of His Spirit, we become more and more who we are destined to be. Your "taproot" needs to take root in the loving heart of God who is both your true Father and Mother.

> *...And I pray that you, being rooted and established in love, may have power, together with all the saints, to grasp how wide and long and high and deep is the love of Christ, and to know this love that surpasses knowledge—that you may be filled to the measure of all the fullness of God* (Ephesians 3:17-19).

That's where the deep nurturing and life-giving water flows from. The Scripture says that drought can come, but your leaves will remain green, and your life will still bear fruit, because your roots are established in an intimate relationship with God, and so His life and leading will flow to you even in dry places.

> *Blessed are those whose strength is in You, who have set their hearts on pilgrimage. As they pass through the Valley of Baca, they make it a place of springs; the autumn rains also cover it with pools. They go from strength to strength, till each appears before God in Zion* (Psalm 84:5-7).

ENDNOTES

1. The love of God is foolishness. This is meant to call forth the joy and mirth of God.

2. Henri Nouwen, *In the Name of Jesus* (New York, NY: Crossroad, 2001), 58-60.

Chapter Nine

HOW THEN SHALL WE LIVE?

And now here's my secret, a very simple secret:
It is only with the heart that one can see rightly;
what is essential is invisible to the eye.

—Antoine de Saint-Exupéry, *The Little Prince*

...the people who know their God will display
strength and take action.

—Daniel 11:32 NASB

I have a friend from Switzerland. The Swiss pride themselves on being very precise and logical in their thinking. The expression "built like a Swiss watch" says a lot about what the Swiss pride themselves in. My friend is an auto technician and he is very skilled at his trade. He can give "life" to a "dead" car, but knowing how to fix things is not what gives a person life. Even repairing a person's body is not a source of life. You could be the greatest heart surgeon in the world, but if you don't know the love of God and don't know how to give love to and receive love from people, what are you? The Scripture says if I am able to speak in the tongues of men and angels but do not have love, I am nothing (see 1 Cor. 13:1). My Swiss friend is much more to me than what he does. What he does is fix cars; what he is, however, is a loved child of God, a husband, a father, and a friend.

Some very intelligent people understand the laws of economics, physics, biology, and sociology, and they can accumulate great wealth, solve many of the world's technological, health, and social problems, and, in many cases, do quite a bit of good in the world. Yet if they have no ability to love or to receive love, then they have no life in them—no knowledge of how to be a father, a mother, a friend…the human being that God created them to be! They have put their knowledge to use profitably, yet knowledge by itself does not make a person able to give and receive love and therefore life.

I need to point out that I believe that knowledge can and does help us love each other effectively; however, it is not of itself a source of love or life. It is perhaps a river bed…but not the river! God put the tree of knowledge in the center of paradise, the Garden of Eden, to show us that knowledge, law, and the order and structure they provide are a foundational part of our existence. However, Scripture tells us that you cannot reach for the tree of knowledge to receive life. If you do, you will die. God wants us to be a tree of life, rooted and established in His love. The roots of the tree of the knowledge of good and evil are in "self" and the knowledge and performance that self can attain. If we feed from this tree, self-love becomes our god—an insatiable condemning god that fears man, not the eternal Father—and the image of who we are is distorted. God is love…

> *This is the first and greatest commandment. And the second is like it: "Love your neighbor as yourself"* (Matthew 22:38-39).

The negative and opposite of Love is self-love. If we are to live in the image of He who is Love, we must live from and toward someone outside of ourselves. The primary object of our love is God, and then our fellow man. This is the great commandment…and the second! We were created for this purpose.

STARVING FOR ATTENTION AND CONTROL

Anorexia is for the most part a performance disease. The condition is found mostly among women and most often begins in adolescence.

According to mental health experts, the *feelings during adolescence* of being overwhelmed and powerless can bring about a desire to maintain control in some realm of life, such as control of body weight. Being in total control of what enters the mouth can give an adolescent a feeling of powerfulness. Thus the period of adolescence may be when anorexia first arises.

Many anorexics come from good families. Their parents are usually very successful and often lovingly desire the best for their children and go to great lengths to provide the very best for them. They are the kind of parents who, when their child comes home with a grade of 90 on an exam, give praise but often with the encouragement that next time she (or he) could aim higher and do better. This may be done with the sincere desire for their child to reach her highest potential. However, too often and unwittingly, the subtle message that is inculcated into the child's subconscious mind is that, in this world, you have to be the best at what you do to have value. So as the little girl is growing up, she begins to think, "If I am going to have value, I must do better—I must learn everything they teach me. I must learn to read, do math, play the piano, sing and dance, and so on. Only then will I have value—and then I will be loved and appreciated."

At some point, many of these girls begin to think that no matter how well they do, it is somehow never good enough. Even if they score 100 percent, they still feel in their heart that it is not good enough. This thinking begins to creep into every part of their life. They feel that they are not clever enough, not smart enough, not beautiful enough, and they begin to feel overwhelmed and powerless. This feeling of powerlessness and being out of control drives them to take control back in perhaps the only area that they feel is still under their control—what they do and do not put in their mouths. Compounding this disease is the message that society and the media has broadcast, that extreme thinness in women is desirable, attractive, and successful. So these young girls decide that this is an area under their control and the thinner they can get, the more attractive, desirable, and successful they will be. It is as if they have slowly hypnotized themselves into this extreme behavior. The eating disorder is merely a symptom of the real underlying problem. They feel overwhelmed, powerless, and that nothing about them is good enough. Why? Because if we feed from the tree of knowledge—and therefore performance—for meaning and value, we are eating fruit that cannot give or nourish life and, just like the anorexic, we starve!

SUSAN

Susan was a young woman in a YWAM missions training school. When everyone else went to bed around 10:00 p.m. she would kneel by her bedside and pray until well after midnight. Before she went to sleep, she would set her alarm clock so that she would wake up at 5:00 a.m. Upon awakening, she would read her Bible and pray more. She felt that this would please God. Every spare moment of her time, she was either reading the Bible or praying. She felt that she could never do enough to repay God for His goodness to her. She seemed to suffer from a kind of spiritual anorexia, starving herself of many needs in order to get more and more control of her life and therefore make herself worthy of God's love.

I asked her to tell me about her parents. She told me that her father, who was a pastor, was the most wonderful man in the whole world. He was always working for God, putting in many extra hours, up at the crack of dawn every day to pray and meet with God and serve Him. She told me that her father could never do enough for God and that he lived simply to please God and set a good example for his family and flock to follow. She had learned her way of life from her daddy. However it was also evident that she had a lack of unconditional maternal nurturing as a woman. I knew it would take a revelation from God in order to free Susan from the slave mentality and bondage she was living under. She could not believe that God simply loved her and valued her as His child. She had become like a trained dog that must perform well to win "Best in Show" and thereby please its master. She had been jumping through spiritual hoops as it were, thinking that she could earn value with God and win God's approval. Nothing she did, however, seemed to satisfy the longing and hunger in her heart to know and experience the love of the Father. She had the mentality of a slave, and no doubt, it broke the heart of the Father who wanted her for His beloved child.

As I prayed with Susan, God gave her revelation that enabled her to see that the Father's love did not depend on her performance. The difficult thing was for her to see that her earthly father had been mistaken and as such needed to be forgiven. When the Holy Spirit enabled her to do this, she was able to experience the love and grace of God wonderfully and unconditionally communicated to her through the good news of Jesus. It is understanding the nature of God's forgiveness that sets us free and opens the door to a new way of serving. Susan's journey was from slavery to a wrong concept of a Father who must be pleased to entering the exquisite energizing joy of becoming His truly beloved and cherished child.

If we derive our value and therefore our identity from performance, it will drive us toward an unhealthy desire for more knowledge and more performance. We will study and strive in order to achieve more in the hope that more knowledge and ability will give us significance and enable us to find meaning in life, or at least satisfaction in life. We frantically learn more and even compete with one another so that we can be better, and thereby make ourselves valuable to God and earn His love. Tragically, many are taught these very ideas in church! (In reality, we perform best when we act out of the sheer love and joy of God or a thing we are doing. We do best when we least think about ourselves and how well we are doing!)

PAUL THE APOSTLE

Before his conversion, Paul, the ultimate Pharisee, was bent on getting everything perfectly right. This was to be accomplished by following the laws and tradition of his people. He had the knowledge—he had been to Pharisee school—he was the best of the best, yet somehow it did not give him life or enable him to see. Nevertheless, he continued to pursue moral perfection, and when the very Life of Heaven came down to earth, he missed it! Wow! Paul the Pharisee did not know God and failed to recognize Him when He came. The Scriptures tell us that Jesus Himself is the way, the truth, and the life. But Paul thought he knew the truth through his knowledge of the Scriptures. His knowledge of the law was perfect—and the law came from God! Yet it did not give him life. Knowledge gives structure and order for life, and in doing so, it is most essential. However, it is relationship that gives life. The law and all it represents can never be done away with. Jesus told us it will always be there. After his conversion, Paul understood the law in its proper context. God had shown him a higher law, the law of the Spirit and life in Jesus.

So…who are you? What do you think makes you valuable? Is it what you can do, or is it that you have seen that God loves you and gave His life for you? Do you derive your identity from eating the fruit of the tree of life by putting your roots down into intimate friendship with God? Or do you seek significance in some way by eating from the tree of the knowledge of good and evil? God doesn't want you to be a tree of knowledge with roots stuck in lifeless and empty performance. He wants so much more for us! Jesus prayed in John 17:3:

> *Now this is eternal life: that they may know You, the only true God, and Jesus Christ, whom You have sent.*

He gave His life to achieve this!

THE WAY OF JESUS

Jesus told the story of the prodigal son. What a story! Here is a guy who broke all the rules. He had failed in every way. For all his stupidity, he ends up living in a pig sty eating pig's food. In Jesus' day this was as low as you could sink (pigs were considered unclean to the Jews). He was in a foreign country eating with pigs. He had become an outcast, the poorest of the poor, the scum of the earth. Then there is the father in the story, who with longing tears and a broken heart full of love says by his actions, "You are precious to me beyond words." He waits every day with longing hope that this son will return. When he finally does return home, a broken and helpless beggar, the father calls for a great celebration feast. He calls for a robe for his son and a ring for his finger. All of us, at times, find ourselves like the prodigal son, overwhelmed by how our Father loves us. It is His great desire that we learn to live in and from the love He has for us.

We are so valued and loved that Jesus gave His own life for our ransom. That's who you really are. You are loved and precious beyond anything you can think or imagine. You are God's child—that is what gives you value. He created you, and you are infinitely valuable to Him. Whether you are in a state of grace or in a state of disgrace and sin, He will always love you (this should never be an excuse for sin!). This will never change. Hopefully such love, once seen, will not be ignored or abused!

We have value because we belong to God. We are created in His image; we are His sons and daughters. A new baby cannot do much: perhaps make noise, wake you up all night, make messy diapers, and stink up the place. Generally, a baby creates a significant amount of unpredictable chaos. Despite all this, the vast majority of fathers and mothers absolutely love their children more than anything else on earth. We need revelation about this in regard to being God's child. Spiritually most days we are all probably like little babies making a glorious mess of many things! I can imagine God having to bear with the stench that comes from the stupid and selfish things we do. Despite this He loves us desperately and will not leave us.

THE PARABLE OF THE PEPPERONI PIZZA

Enrico Bodoni sat down in a pizza restaurant one day...an establishment operated by two of his sons. When the pizza entrepreneurs heard he was there, they prepared their best Pepperoni Special and sent it to their father. But soon, the word filtered back to the kitchen that Mr. Bodoni was not touching his pizza. The Bodoni brothers were astounded and marched out to the table. "Papa, we noticed you're not eating your pizza."

"No, I suppose I'm not," was the even reply.

"Bodoni Brothers' pizza is the best pizza in town," said the pizza men. "Everyone says so."

"I've heard that around the neighborhood," said their father.

"We put a lot of time and effort into that pizza."

"I know."

"The ingredients were the very best."

"So I see."

The pizza chefs leaned in closer to the table. "Papa, you're embarrassing us. You know, sitting here in front of all our other customers, and not touching your pizza."

"Sorry."

Finally, the brothers threw up their hands in exasperation. "So, why aren't you eating your pizza?"

"I don't like pizza. Never have."

The brothers Bodoni were flabbergasted. "What do mean you don't like pizza? Of course you like pizza! You come in here all the time! If you didn't like pizza, why would you come to a pizza restaurant?"

The father replied kindly, "I don't come in here because I like pizza. I come in here because I like you."[1]

God is not concerned about performance apart from relationship. He is primarily concerned about being in an intimate relationship with us, His children. I like to perform well. It is fun and fulfilling up to a point, but it's not who I am, and it does not have lasting value and significance. Performance is at the "peripheral edge" of who I am; but at the center of who I am, I am a loved child of my Father and, because of that one thing, I have value beyond measure. The Holy Spirit needs to enable us to see this so we can become whole men and women, released from the curse of the

Fall, which causes us to grasp for power to find value and significance. This latter kind of activity is likely to produce a false and distorted masculinity and femininity in us.

My Sons

My wife and I have wonderful sons who are very bright and intelligent. One of our boys, while growing up in Africa, was consistently at the top of his class. When he graduated from middle school, he won every academic achievement. I wrote him a letter afterward in which I said, "I am very proud that you did so well, but I want you to know that that is not why I love you or why you are precious to me. Even if you were at the bottom of the class, I would love you exactly the same. You would be just as precious and valuable to me. My love for you does not depend on how well you do. You are my son—that's why I love you."

I went on to explain that God loved him in the same way. The letter was written to counteract the message the world would send my son. This world with its ways would tell him that he is valuable because of his performance. If he believed that lie, he may no doubt start to pursue performance as the source of life, significance, and identity. I am very proud of my sons and their amazing gifts and achievements; however, I love them because they are my sons.

Something to Do

A Prayer:

> *Lord Jesus, we thank You for the picture of the two trees in the Bible and what they help us understand about ourselves and You. Your dream for every person is to be a tree of life with roots that go down into the love of the Father in Heaven. Lord Jesus, I pray that You help my roots go down into You. Give me an identity that comes from knowing You and the love You have for me. Please take me on*

the journey of revealing to me my true name that is known only to You. Enable me to grow into the real man/woman You created me to be. Teach me to listen for Your voice and take action as you direct me. Amen!

ENDNOTE

1. Charles Mclean, "Parable of the Pizza" freethefrogs.blogspot .com/2009/05/parable-of-pizza.html, (Accessed June 10, 2009).

Chapter Ten

Rooted and Established in God

The question of Jesus' joyfulness is not trivial for this reason:
Prayer is personal response to loving Presence. When the Jesus
of our journey is the smiling Christ, when we respond to His
whispered word, "I'm wild about you," the process of inner healing
can begin. He heals us of our absorption in ourselves—where we
take ourselves too seriously, where the days and nights revolve
around us, our heartaches and hiatal hernias, our problems
and frustrations. His smile allows us to distance ourselves from
ourselves and see ourselves in perspective as we really are.

—Brennan Manning, *The Signature of Jesus*[1]

For this is what the Lord says: "I will extend peace to her like a
river, and the wealth of nations like a flooding stream; you will
nurse and be carried on her arm and dandled on her knees. As a
mother comforts her child, so will I comfort you; and you will be
comforted over Jerusalem."

—Isaiah 66:12-13

*We have come to share in Christ if we hold firmly till the
end the confidence we had at first.*

—Hebrews 3:14

TAKING IT IN

THERE is an African parable in which God gives to a child a mother
in order to feed him, including the breast of the mother to feed from,
and the milk in the mother's breast to feed on. However, the child
must learn to suck the milk from the mother's breast if he is going to receive
the nourishment and life that is so freely and lovingly offered.

Even a "helpless" little baby, feeling hunger, must actively take in
or feed on the nourishment offered in order to live and grow. God never
intended that we should be force-fed! In all things in life we were created
with a divine capacity to respond in free and joyful obedience. God does
not force Himself on us! That would be like the physical equivalent of rape.
God desires a tender expression of free and responsive love.

God provides all we need for life and growth, but His provision will do
us no good if we do not learn, like the infant, to suck the nourishment from
the breast. We must respond and receive these things into our hearts! We
must, from our hearts, desire to grow. We must want to change. We must
want to be different. We must want to be healed. A baby cannot just lie
there wanting something and do nothing about it. He must first cry out his
need and then receive the nourishment offered. If not, such a child would
soon die. It is important that we listen to God and receive the words He
speaks and respond to the convictions (never condemnation) He sends. We
cannot just lie there and expect God to do everything. God actually does
do everything, but He expects us to use our God-given free will to pursue
our God-given longing for Him, cry out to Him, and actively receive Him.
Receiving His thoughts is not passive; it takes an active act of will, faith,
and submission, yet it is still the "act" of receiving. God does all the rest.

When God initiates with us, we need to respond. He is not going to dominate or force us. When God is extending grace, we need to receive it and respond to it with the faith He gives us. If we do not, we will not changed healed and grow. As the eagle drops off the cliff, then responds to the wind and is lifted up, so are we to respond to the power and love of God.

Faith—a Way to Respond

The only faculty by which we can approach and respond to God is faith. By actively believing and trusting God, we grasp hold of and take in everything He desires to give us. However, even our ability to respond is a gift of grace from the Father. What God says to us and does in us becomes for us the milk and bread and meat of life that changes us and matures us into the spiritual adults He created us to be.

Walking Out of Our Wounds

All people have problems. All people have internal wounds. All people are broken. This is the condition of our fallen nature. It is a condition of imprisonment caused by choosing knowledge, performance, and self as one's gods, only to find oneself imprisoned by the angry little "self" gods and the fear of man that self-centeredness produces. Only God can free us from this prison. He opens the prison door and He provides a way for us to walk out—but God is not going to push us out the door. He is the One who is at work in us making us willing and able to obey...but He is not going to force us or control us (see Phil. 2:13). He will break open the prison door and show us the way out, but we must do the "walk" of receiving. God is initiating. He offers us His love, His peace, His joy. We only need to respond and receive the gift. Receiving God's gifts is very much like learning to walk. A baby must master the coordination required to walk, the balance required to walk, and develop the muscles and strength required to walk. However, once a baby has had their first "sense" of walking, they can't practice enough! They become dedicated to mastering this new level of living.

Sometimes a child is reared in a way that makes him or her dependent, and so the child never really grows up. This is not what God wants for us. As our eternal parent God is close to us and He is with us always. When we need it, God will carry us, but for the most part we must learn to walk when God wants us to walk. We must learn to drink in the milk of God's words to us—the love and the grace that He gives us. We must respond to all He says to our hearts and, by doing so, grow and become strong in Him. God gives a lot of grace, but we need to learn to walk and live in that grace. We are not robots, for God has given us a will. We are not animals, for God has given us a spirit. And we are not slaves, for God has given us a free will over what we choose. He loves us and desires us to freely choose Him and love Him also. Otherwise, instead of being created in the likeness of God, our fate would have been that of the robot, a mere animal, or a slave.

Being a Tree of Life

There are so many scriptural "tree pictures" in the Bible. The Bible uses the tree as a symbol for a person and his or her identity or, as I sometimes like to call it, his "who-ness."

> Psalm 1:1-3: *Blessed is the man who does not walk in the counsel of the wicked or stand in the way of sinners or sit in the seat of mockers. But his delight is in the law of the Lord, and on His law he meditates day and night. He is **like a tree** planted by streams of water, which yields its fruit in season and whose leaf does not wither. Whatever he does prospers.*

> Proverbs 11:30: *The fruit of the righteous is a tree of life.*

> Ezekiel 47:12: *Fruit trees of all kinds will grow on both banks of the river. Their leaves will not wither, nor will*

their fruit fail. Every month they will bear, because the water from the sanctuary flows to them. Their fruit will serve for food and their leaves for healing.

Ephesians 3:17-19: *So that Christ may dwell in your hearts through faith. And I pray that you, being **rooted and established** in love, may have power, together with all the saints, to grasp how wide and long and high and deep is the love of Christ, and to know this love that surpasses knowledge—that you may be filled to the measure of all the fullness of God.*

Paul prays that our roots and our foundation would be in God's love, and that we would be able, together with the saints, our brothers and sisters, to measure the height and depth of God's love. Sometimes the Holy Spirit chooses to communicate the love of God to an individual in the context of the gathered saints. The grace and love of God is frequently channeled through the human faces of the gathered family about us. When our roots go down into this love, we will be strengthened and grow into real men and women. We need to actively drink in the milk of that love and fully receive it in our hearts. Then we will be empowered to do the things that God is calling us to. The passage in Ephesians goes on to say that as we do this we will be filled with the complete and full nature of God.

THE HUMAN BODY

The skeletal structure of the human body provides a brilliant illustration of the tree of life and the tree of knowledge and the concept of masculinity and femininity. Life for the human body does not come from the bones. Bones provide structure for the body, and the skeleton gives that structure. However, it is the marrow inside the bones that provides life for the body. Marrow is a soft liquid substance generated in the center of the bones. It is significant that this source of life is to be found inside the very part of the body that provides strong and firm structure. Blood cells are made from the marrow, and it is the blood that carries life to the rest of the body. This illustration of the intimate relationship of the skeletal structure with the life-giving marrow is a beautiful picture of the marriage that exists between the structure of life and life itself, form and matter, masculine and feminine—and, of course, the two trees growing along side each other in the center of the garden. These illustrations help us understand both the polar differences and the essential relationship between the two trees, which in turn help us understand the polarity that exists between the masculine and the feminine and yet the essential relationship between the two.

There is truth here that we must see with the eyes of our imagination if we are to be spiritual people who worship the Father in Spirit and in truth. It is our relationship with God and our relationship with each other that are the "marrow"—the essence of life itself! When man was separated from God, he was left apart from the Source of life and alone with the law—that is, the rules and structure. Jesus brought Heaven back to us—He joined the waning stream of our life back to its Spring. If we are not connected to the Source of our life, then as we live life we progressively run out of marrow until all that is left are dry bones—emptiness.

In Revelation 22:1-5, John tells us there is the tree of life growing on both sides of the river…and that there is no more curse:

> *Then the angel showed me the river of the water of life, as clear as crystal, flowing from the throne of God and of the Lamb down the middle of the great street of the city. On each side of the river stood **the tree of life,** bearing twelve crops of fruit, yielding its fruit every month. And the leaves of the tree are for the healing of the nations. **No longer will there be any curse.** The throne of God and of the Lamb will be in the city, and His servants will serve Him. They will see His face, and His name will be on their foreheads. There will be no more night. They will not need the light of a lamp or the light of the sun, for the Lord God will give them light. And they will reign for ever and ever.*

Jesus said. *"I have not come to do away with the law, but to fulfill the law"* (see Matt. 5:17). For this reason, in Revelation 22 there is only one tree—the tree of life. What happened to the other tree? It is perhaps taken up into the tree of life and the two have become one. The tree of knowledge (the law) is fulfilled within the vibrant health of the tree of life (lives filled with the presence and love of God).

THE LAW A CURSE?

In Galatians, Paul calls the law a curse. How can something that comes from God be a curse? Think of a wheelchair. A wheelchair is a blessing that can be a means of getting about for someone who has lost the ability to walk. When I see a wheelchair I think it a good thing, but I also see it as a sad curse. I would rather see legs walk as they were created to! When Adam fell, we all lost the good of God's loving presence and the grace that flows from friendship with Him. We were left as orphans, alone with the law to help us get along. When we could no longer see or hear the source of our life, the law became for us the wheelchair we needed to enable us to manage life in separation from the Life of Heaven. Since we chose independence and being god for ourselves then we had better have some good rules to do it with! If there is no intimate communion with God then there better be the law and our knowledge of it to help us along.

We know that mere obedience to the law does not give us communion with God. The story of Paul's conversion teaches us this. It is Christ who does it! When Jesus comes to live inside us, the essential thing He wants to accomplish is restoring the intimate fellowship between us, Himself, and the Father. He wants to teach us again to hear Him and see Him in the same way He heard and saw the Father. He wants to restore the "image" of the Father in His children.

> *Jesus gave them this answer: "I tell you the truth, the Son can do nothing by Himself; He can do only what He sees His Father doing, because whatever the Father does the Son also does. For the Father loves the Son and shows*

Him all He does. Yes, to your amazement He will show
Him even greater things... " (John 5:19-20).

In John 3:3 Jesus declared, *"I tell you the truth, no one can **see** the*
kingdom of God unless he is born again. " When the grace and the love of
God truly come alive to our hearts then we will begin to do the right thing
without even thinking about the law. We simply begin to *see*. We are caught
up in the goodness of God. It is the leading of the Spirit that makes us into
sons of God! He longs to teach us to dance to the rhythm of His heart. This
is God's desire for us—this is what will heal our fallen and broken identities and make of us real men and women. Our roots and foundation will be
in love and not striving to perform or please. We will listen to and obey the
voice of Jesus simply because we are caught up in the great enchantment
of His eternal love and beauty. To enter such a place with God is the very
purpose of salvation. Such a person could almost forget that the law exists.
When you are obeying God Himself, living in His love and following the
direction of the Holy Spirit, the law is fulfilled. This is what it means to
be a tree of life: *"...to know God and to know Jesus whom He sent"* (John
17:3).

Do not think that I have come to abolish the Law or the
Prophets; I have not come to abolish them but to fulfill
them (Matthew 5:17).

ENDNOTE

1. Brennan Manning, (Colorada Springs, CO: Multnomah Books,
    2004).

Chapter Eleven

FRIENDSHIP WITH GOD

*"She had seen the face of God…and that face was Love—love
like a mother's, only deeper, tenderer, lovelier, stronger. She could
not recall what she had seen or how she had known it; but the
conviction remained that she had seen His face,
and it was infinitely beautiful."*

—George MacDonald, *The Maiden's Bequest*

*"If I speak in the tongues of men and of angels, but have not love,
I am only a resounding gong or a clanging cymbal. If I have the
gift of prophecy and can fathom all mysteries and all knowledge,
and if I have a faith that can move mountains, but have not love,
I am nothing. If I give all I possess to the poor and surrender my
body to the flames, but have not love, I gain nothing."*

—1 Corinthians 13:1-3

IN Second Corinthians chapter 3 there is a marvelous passage that portrays the difference between the Old and New Covenants. The law, which is the essence of the Old Covenant, was given to Moses. With it came a sense of the glory and presence of God shining on the face of Moses. When he came down the mountain, he had to cover his face with a veil. The people could not look at him because of the brightness of the glory of God shining in his face. He had been with God! The "veil" over his face represents, according to Paul, the separation that exists between God and humans because of what happened in the Garden of Eden. Paul also indicates that this veil represents the Law. In Christ this veil is taken away! We are now enabled by the power of the Holy Spirit to encounter God Himself and are thereby daily transformed into His marvelous image. It is a wonderful passage…

> *Now if the ministry that brought death, which was engraved in letters on stone, came with glory, so that the Israelites could not look steadily at the face of Moses because of its glory, fading though it was, will not the ministry of the Spirit be even more glorious? If the ministry that condemns men is glorious, how much more glorious is the ministry that brings righteousness! For what was glorious has no glory now in comparison with the surpassing glory. And if what was fading away came with glory, how much greater is the glory of that which lasts! Therefore, since we have such a hope, we are very bold. We are not like Moses, who would put a veil over his face to keep the Israelites from gazing at it while the radiance was fading away. But their minds were made dull, for to this day the same veil remains when the old covenant is read. It has not been removed, because only in Christ is it taken away. Even to this day when Moses is read, a veil covers their hearts. But whenever anyone turns to the Lord, the veil is taken away. Now the Lord is the Spirit, and where the Spirit of the Lord is, there is freedom. And we, who with unveiled faces all reflect the Lord's glory, are being transformed into His likeness with ever-increasing glory, which comes from the Lord, who is the Spirit* (2 Corinthians 3:7-18).

THE EXAMPLE OF JESUS

Jesus Himself is our primary model of someone who derived His identity from friendship and intimacy with the Father. He is the new Adam—that is, the "new man!"

In John chapter 5, some of the Pharisees were challenging Jesus as to who He was and where He got His authority. He had just healed someone on the Sabbath and was accused by some Pharisees because it was against the law to "work" on the Sabbath. Usually people (we are all recovering Pharisees!) have been granted authority because they've graduated from some school, a course of training, an apprenticeship, or had experience at something or other. They have in a sense "grown up" and learned the ropes and gained knowledge of the rules of some system or other. They are qualified to "perform." This is mostly where people seek authority and significant identity in the ways of this fallen world (i.e., a tree of knowledge). Jesus cut right across this claiming that He had no authority "of His own" but that He received authority directly from a direct relationship with His Father (a tree of life). He was the Son of God!

He claimed that He did only what He saw the Father doing—as He heard the Father He would judge and make decisions. He said that what He did was right, because He did not seek His own will, but the will of the Father who sent Him (see John 5:19,30). His entire identity—that is, everything He was and did including His authority flowed out of close communication and collaboration with the Father.

Who Jesus is cannot be separated from the Father. He said, "I and the Father are one." What a fantastically wonderful picture of real and true identity! Jesus' way of life is the Father's plan for everyone. He provides us with the pattern for true men and women alike. His command is that we follow Him in the enabling power of the promised Holy Spirit. Hallelujah!

> *Jesus gave them this answer: "I tell you the truth, the Son can do nothing by Himself; He can do only what He sees His Father doing, because whatever the Father does the Son also does. For the Father loves the Son and shows*

Him all He does. Yes, to your amazement He will show Him even greater things than these. For just as the Father raises the dead and gives them life, even so the Son gives life to whom He is pleased to give it....By Myself I can do nothing; I judge only as I hear, and My judgment is just, for I seek not to please Myself but Him who sent Me (John 5:19-21,30).

God's desire for all of us is to have our roots and identity in His love for us. He wants us to be like Jesus...to be discipled in the way that He lived His life on earth. God's plan for us is to learn to hear His heart and from it gain a righteousness that is revealed and comes from trusting Him.

In our journey through this world, we are all learning the same lessons. Not one of us is better than the other. The Spirit is presently at work in all God's children to enable us to let go of the false sense of "grown up-ness"—a power and control that come from a wrong kind of grasping and clinging to knowledge—and to help us return to the childlike simplicity of devotion to Jesus. We are to hear and follow the voice of a Shepherd. In the context of such a relationship, knowledge is invaluable and has a right place. What I am saying is by no means a vendetta against knowledge. It is an attempt to pull down the idol that we have made of it and redeem it. I am a great advocate of education and equipping people and teaching them to think. Nothing is "wrong" until it takes the place of God! When Jesus is at the center all things have their proper place.

A Jewish Story

There is a story of a little Jewish boy who had a hard time learning to get things right. Each day he would leave a trail of disaster behind him. He could never brush his teeth without making a mess, and he was an impossible problem at school, always getting things wrong. His parents were at the end of themselves not knowing what to do. What he liked was to come home and play by himself in the trees and by the stream behind his house.

In desperation his parents told him that if he did not change for the better, they were going to take the ultimate and terrifying step of taking him to see the Rabbi. This last resort to engender obedience sounded like the most frightful thing to the small boy. But still, even this threat somehow was not able to help him get things right.

And so, in time the fateful day came. One morning his parents dressed him in uncomfortable clothes and then set off to see the Rabbi. The boy was stricken with fright. At the synagogue they took him into a large room full of books and a strange and holy smell...before him sat the great bearded Rabbi. The boy heard nothing but the frantic beating of his little heart as his parents told the sad story of the struggle to get this child to be obedient. When the boy's parents were done, the Rabbi sat in silent thought for a moment and then did the worst possible thing. He asked the parents to go and leave the boy alone with him. He then silently beckoned the boy with his finger to come to him. With growing terror the boy slowly edged his way across the great chasm toward the old man. When he was close enough the rabbi gently reached out his big old arms and drew the child gently and securely into his bosom. There he stood for what seemed a terrifying eternity...firmly held against the great breast of the Rabbi.

At first the little fellow thought he would simply die, but after a while he became aware of a mysterious and captivating sound. It was a sound like no other he had ever heard. As he listened to the rhythm of the Rabbi's great heart, he slowly forgot his fear and began to relax. He stayed for a long while in the warm embrace of the Rabbi lost in the rhythmic sound that had captivated his imagination. In time, the Rabbi gently released him and silently indicated for him to go and call his parents. When they came in, he told them that he had had a good talk with the boy and that everything was going to be all right.

The next morning he got up and somehow brushed his teeth without messing up. He went to school and there he began to learn. He came home and went off to play in the trees and by the river he loved. There he continued to learn from the trees, birds, and flowers, and from the stream as it ran over rocks and into quiet pools...

This parable tells the story of many thousands who have come to know the love of the Father.

The essence of the good news that came to us in Jesus is that the Father has removed everything that separates us from Him and reached out to take us into His loving and eternal embrace. His plan is to captivate us with the sound of His beating heart. He wants to intoxicate us with His love and the goodness that flows from Him. He knows that when we hear and understand His heartbeat all will be different. When we learn to move to the rhythm of the heartbeat of Heaven we will be transformed—we will be good. That is the sneak plan of Heaven. We will come to know salvation in all His fullness and so be healed and eternally delivered from ourselves. He will write His laws on our hearts and with joy we will draw water from the wells of salvation!

All this is the work of the Holy Spirit in the lives of those who believe. It is essentially a work of revelation. We are told in the first chapter of the letter to the Romans that in the good news of Jesus there is a righteousness that comes from God...and is revealed...and is by faith from first to last (see Rom. 1:17). When He has completed the work He has begun in us we will no longer be living out of striving to perform. There will be no more thinking, *Am I okay? Am I doing enough? Will He be pleased with my performance?* We will have come to know that it doesn't depend simply on what we do but on how we respond by faith to His loving initiative and leading.

When you encounter the eternal love out of an intimate experience of God, it changes you—it's like supernatural "holy" magic. The mystery of the goodness of God will begin to be revealed inside you. Holiness will become a fountain of energy and life that has its source in the One who alone is holy. You will simply know what is right and will do what is right. Why? Because in your spirit you are in tune with God, one with Him and living in His love, trusting Him and dancing to the rhythm of the great Heart of Heaven. Christ in me the hope of glory...!

It is childlike trust that makes the connection. Without faith it is impossible to please God! This is why the New Testament says we must believe.

Our response of faith is how we receive the nurturing and life-giving milk of God's presence and love. God says, "I love you"—believe it and in faith learn to follow the leading of the Spirit. It is thus we learn the reason why we were created...to be filled with the divine and eternal Presence!

RIGHTEOUSNESS THAT COMES FROM GOD

Paul tells us in his letter to the Romans of a righteousness that comes from God Himself (see Rom. 1:17). Righteousness that comes from obeying the law is self-righteousness. This is the righteousness Paul had before his conversion. He obeyed all of the law and the religious tradition, but somehow completely missed God. In the Gospel of Jesus, there is a goodness that comes to us from God Himself!

The next thing Paul says is that this righteousness comes by revelation. If something is revealed it means that it did not merely come from intellectual ability to figure it out, nor from our emotions. Nor is it merely imagined. When the Spirit gives revelation it may well come to us in our intellects, emotions, and/or imaginations. It is usually quite unexpected and spontaneous. When God reveals something to us He does not always use words. It is often more like you seeing rather than hearing and it comes inside you—a joy and a love that is like a spring that bubbles up and you suddenly know what to do or say. It is like wisdom that "shines" in your heart. Spontaneously you find yourself knowing what God is saying and can joyfully find yourself in the midst of His will like being carried by the current of a river. God doesn't just reveal things to you...more often than not He reveals things inside you. It is a beautiful thing when this happens. Suddenly and naturally you find that by His grace you are walking with God in the power of His Spirit. There is a righteousness that comes from God and is revealed!

Paul goes on to tell us that all of this happens *"by faith from first to last"* (Rom. 1:17). Life with God is all about faith. Faith is the means by which we drink in the life and goodness of the Father. To trust is the one thing we can and must do. God reveals His righteousness to us and we receive it and live it by faith. When we, by faith, receive what God gives, it has power to change us and make us good from the inside out!

All the law in the world does not have the power to change us and make us good. The work of the law is to tell us what sin is and to let us know that we are guilty of it. The law in fact leads us to Christ:

> Therefore the Law has become our tutor to lead us to Christ, that we may be justified by faith (Galatians 3:24 NASB).

When Paul says this, the word used in the Greek for tutor, *paidagogos,* is referring to what in the United States is called a truant officer. A truant officer is somebody who is appointed by a school district to go about seeing if he can spot a child that is not at school. He has authority to confront and do whatever it takes to get the child back in school. Once the child is in school, the truant officer's work is done. In terms of the Gospel it is within a personal and real relationship with Jesus that we belong, listening to and learning to follow the heart of God. If we sin, we step outside of the "school" of the Spirit, and the law again has authority to come after us and herd us like a sheepdog back to Jesus.

So...if I sin and then perceive the law coming after me, I can run back to the cross, the place where I can repent and be forgiven, to the very thing that enables me to walk humbly and obediently back into relationship with God. What wonderful grace! Once I am returned to Jesus, I can respectfully look in the face of the "truant officer" without fear. He cannot touch me because I am in Jesus and Jesus is in me and I am no longer living under His authority. Some have seen such marvelous grace as an opportunity to sin all the more. What an awful abuse of God's tender grace! *"What shall we say then? Are we to continue in sin so that grace may increase? May it never be!..."* (Rom. 6:1-2 NASB). In true English style, J.B. Philips translates the last bit of this passage with, *"What a ghastly thought!"*

The law only has authority when I am out of relationship with the Holy Spirit. Paul tells us that we are not under the law but under the Spirit. Jesus said, *"My sheep listen to My voice; I know them and they follow Me"* (John 10:27).

> *But if you are led by the Spirit, you are not under law* (Galatians 5:18).

> *My sheep listen to My voice; I know them, and they follow Me* (John 10:27).

So we learn to respond to the leading of the Spirit and receive a righteousness that comes from God and is by faith and faith alone. Thus we become the tree of Life that Jesus desires us to be. We are to be His friends!

SOMETHING TO DO

Be still and reflect on the story of the little boy being embraced by the Rabbi. Quietly imagine yourself in the loving embrace of Father God, and listen for what His great heart would say to you. Pray with sure faith that the heart beat of His love for you and His world would become the very rhythm and fabric of your life.

Chapter Twelve

WINGS TO FLY!

"Now this is eternal life: that they may know You, the only true God, and Jesus Christ, whom You have sent."

John 17:3

"Sweet is the lore which Nature brings
our meddling intellect
mis-shapes the beauteous forms of things
we murder to dissect.
Enough of Science and of Art
Close up those barren leaves
come forth, and bring with you a heart
That watches and receives."

— William Wordsworth,
The Tables Turned

GOD did not create us for morality. We were created in order to be filled with the divine presence of God! We are to be filled with the very life and breath of Heaven Himself. This is the purpose of life.

C.S. Lewis, in his essay "Man or Rabbit," likened morality to a very high mountain that only a few elite are able to scale.[1] People like Paul, before his conversion, and Job seemed able to conquer this mountain. The Scriptures indicate that in the case of Paul and Job the ability to obey the law was exemplary but clearly not enough. Despite their peculiar brands of self-righteousness, they missed God and needed to receive mercy and revelation in order to be brought into the relationship of grace and faith for which they were created.

Lewis points out that if you reach the mountain's summit you are likely to die from extreme cold and lack of oxygen. Reaching the summit, Lewis says, is only the beginning. It is only the first step in a far greater journey. To go higher you need wings...you have to learn to fly. You need faith!

Lewis suggests that a man who asks if becoming a Christian would make him a better person shows by his question that he has no real understanding of what Christianity is all about. In the essay he writes of the person who by seeking the moral route would evade a personal meeting with the Creator:

> ....He is like the man who won't go to the doctor when he first feels a mysterious pain, because he is afraid of what the doctor may tell him.

> The man who remains an unbeliever for such reasons is not in a state of honest error. He is in a state of dishonest error, and that dishonesty will spread through all his thoughts and actions: a certain shiftiness, a vague worry in the background, a blunting of his whole mental edge, will result. He has lost his intellectual virginity. Honest rejection of Christ, however mistaken, will be forgiven and healed— *"Whosoever shall speak a word against the Son of Man, it shall be forgiven him."* (Luke 12:10) But to *evade* the Son of Man, to look the other way, to pretend you haven't noticed, to become suddenly absorbed in something on the other side of the street, to leave the receiver off the

telephone because it might be He who was ringing up, to leave unopened certain letters in a strange handwriting because they might be from Him—this is a different matter. You may not be certain yet whether you ought to be a Christian; but you do know you ought to be a man, not an ostrich, hiding its head in the sands.

But still—for intellectual honour has sunk very low in our age—I hear someone whimpering on with his questions. "Will it help me? Will it make me happy? Do you really think I'd be better if I became a Christian?" Well if you must have it, my answer is "Yes." But I don't like giving an answer at all at this stage. Here is a door, behind which, according to some people, the secret of the universe is waiting for you. Either that's true, or it isn't. And if it isn't, then what the door really conceals is simply the greatest fraud, the most colossal "sell" on record. Isn't it obviously the job of every man (that is a man and not a rabbit) to try to find out which, and then to devote his full energies either to serving this tremendous secret or to exposing and destroying this gigantic humbug? Faced with such an issue, can you really remain wholly absorbed in your blessed "moral development"?

All right, Christianity will do you good—a great deal more good than you ever wanted or expected. And the first bit of good it will do you is to hammer into your head (you won't enjoy *that*) the fact that what you have hitherto called "good"—all that about "leading a decent life" and "being kind"—isn't quite the magnificent and all-important affair you supposed. It will teach you that in fact you can't be "good" (not for twenty-four hours) on your own moral efforts. And then it will teach you that even if you were, you still wouldn't have achieved the purpose for which you were created. Mere morality is not the end of life. You were made for something quite different from that. J. S. Mill and Confucius (Socrates was much nearer the reality) simply didn't know what life is about. The people who keep on asking if they can't lead a decent life without Christ, don't know what life is about; if they did they would know that "a decent life" is mere machinery compared with the thing we men are really made for. Morality is indispensable: but the Divine Life, which gives itself to us and which calls us to be gods, intends for us something in which morality will be swallowed up. We are to be re-made. All the rabbit in us is to disappear—the worried, conscientious, ethical rabbit as well as the cowardly and sensual rabbit. We shall bleed and squeal as the handfuls of fur come out; and then, surprisingly, we shall find underneath it all a thing we have never yet imagined: a real man, an ageless god, a son of God strong, radiant, wise, beautiful, and drenched in joy.

When that which is perfect is come, then that which is in part shall be done away. (I Corinthians 13:10) The idea of reaching a good life without Christ is based on a double error. Firstly, we cannot do it; and secondly, in setting up "a good life" as the final goal, we have missed the very point of our existence. Morality is a mountain which we cannot climb by our own efforts; and if we could we should only perish in the ice and unbreathable air of the summit, lacking those wings with which the rest of the journey has to be accomplished. For it is from there that the real ascent begins. The ropes and axes are "done away" and the rest is a matter of flying.[2]

The illustration suggests that if we are ever going to make it, we need a miracle. To live in God and have God live in us is a miracle only the Holy Spirit can give. The forgiveness Jesus made available in dying on the cross makes this miracle possible. It is our faith responding to the work and wind of the Spirit in our life that alone lifts us into a higher place of goodness and holiness where the real life of Heaven begins to dawn within us.

Consider Jesus' prayer in John chapter 17 verses 20 and 21…it is the prayer He was carrying in His heart the very night before He was crucified:

> *My prayer is not for them alone. I pray also for those who will believe in Me through their message, that all of them may be one, Father, just as You are in Me and I am in You. May they also be in us so that the world may believe that You have sent Me.*

The picture of the metamorphosis of a dragonfly speaks to us of the transformation that is needed. At first the dragonfly lives as a wormlike creature in the cool dark world at the bottom of a pool. One bright day it crawls out of the pool onto a rock where it is thoroughly baked and dried by the sun. As the old body that equipped it for living in the muddy world of the pool floor cracks open, the new dragonfly is released. The new creation is for the air and for flight! This is reminiscent of the journey from the Old Testament world of morality to the entirely new dimension of the New Testament world of the Spirit and the life of faith. If we are to know God as Jesus knew the Father we have to leave our old world behind and be completely remade for the new! These two ways of being are *exclusive* of each other. Paul, in speaking of living by the law or by the Spirit, puts it this way:

> *Tell me, you who want to be under the law, are you not aware of what the law says? For it is written that Abraham had two sons, one by the slave woman and the other by the free woman. His son by the slave woman was born in the ordinary way; but his son by the free woman was born as the result of a promise. These things may be taken figuratively, for the women represent two covenants. One covenant is from Mount Sinai and bears children who are to be slaves: This is Hagar.*

Now Hagar stands for Mount Sinai in Arabia and corresponds to the present city of Jerusalem, because she is in slavery with her children. But the Jerusalem that is above is free, and she is our mother. For it is written: "Be glad, O barren woman, who bears no children; break forth and cry aloud, you who have no labor pains; because more are the children of the desolate woman than of her who has a husband."

Now you, brothers, like Isaac, are children of promise. At that time the son born in the ordinary way persecuted the son born by the power of the Spirit. It is the same now.

But what does the Scripture say? "Get rid of the slave woman and her son, for the slave woman's son will never share in the inheritance with the free woman's son." Therefore, brothers, we are not children of the slave woman, but of the free woman (Galatians 4:21-31).

It is for freedom that Christ has set us free. Stand firm, then, and do not let yourselves be burdened again by a yoke of slavery (Galatians 5:1).

ENDNOTES

1. C.S. Lewis *God in the Dock: Essays on Theology and Ethics* (Grand Rapids, MI: Eerdmans Publishing Company, 1994).

2. Ibid.

Chapter Thirteen

THE BONSAI TREE

"I never sat in the company of revelers, never made merry with them; I sat alone because Your hand was on me and You had filled me with indignation. Why is my pain unending and my wound grievous and incurable? Will You be to me like a deceptive brook, like a spring that fails?"

—Jeremiah 15:17-18

THE Japanese have an art form in which they grow miniature trees. These are called bonsai trees. In order to do this they take a baby tree, cut the primary root—that is the taproot—and plant the tree in a small pot with a shallow amount of soil. This restricts growth and causes the tree to develop into a dwarflike miniature. A tree like this never has much inner strength, and as such it is fragile and it needs constant care. This paints a vivid picture of codependence. A friend of mine forgot to care for his bonsai trees for a few days with the result that half of them died. The bonsai tree is fashioned in such a way that it has to remain dependent on a master—or perhaps a system. It never develops a healthy life of its own.

The picture of the bonsai tree correlates to the devil's plan for God's children. He wants to "bonsai" us. God's purpose was that our taproot would go down into His love and that we would grow strong, large, and free, drawing our life, identity, and goodness from friendship with Him.

In the Garden of Eden the devil cut the taproot of the tree we were and we became a tree of knowledge of good and evil. Thus we became tragically stunted and malnourished, dependent on our knowledge of the law in order to maintain a sense of life and identity. God wants us to develop a "life of our own;" however, this is not a license for us to develop an unhealthy *independence!* Balance is always the way to go.

On the Hilo side of the Big Island of Hawaii it rains almost every day of the year. Birds drop seeds of trees onto the lava rock, and because of the excess moisture the trees manage to grow on the rock. Because they take root on the rock these trees become like bonsai trees. They can be all of 30 years old and still be quite small, with the roots creeping along in the cracks on the rocks. They are not able to put down a taproot or get much nutrition. They only just manage to survive because of the frequent rains.

It is similar with human beings. In this fallen world we have all to some extent taken root in dry and rocklike places that have kept us from the rich, deep life-giving soil of God's maternal and paternal love and care. We are neither nurtured nor called into being in the way God had originally planned. Sometimes there is a little good human parental soil in our lives, but underneath there is the lifeless shale of our fallen and performance-oriented world. Many hard rocks cause wounds that separate us from our true selves and friendship with Heaven. Like waifs growing up on a desert island, we are not aware of the extent of our poverty and ills. Those who are color-blind would never know they were color-blind if no one ever made them aware of it! We are not aware of how far we are fallen and how very wounded we are. We grasp for what little life and worth we can get from gaining knowledge and performing in order to be valued.

SEXUAL ORIENTATION

In the same way our understanding of our sexual identity and orientation is shaped by the combination of the "bonsai effect" of past wounds, wrong social conditioning, and then by unfortunate and wrong choices. For the most part, it is my opinion that lesbianism and male homosexuality develop in this way. (Temperament can be a *contributive influence* when certain crucial decisions are made, but I do not believe it to be a major determining factor in the choice made.)

From around the age of 10 through 14 a boy has a great need to attach to and build relationship with his father. This helps him embrace and take in what it means to be a man. Good fathering affirms and calls sons into manhood and imparts to them a sense of confidence and true masculine strength and identity. Many things can get in the way of this. A father could be an excessively angry or depressed man, an alcoholic, or perhaps distant. Some are unfaithful and abandon the care of the family. There are a great number of reasons why a young man might be prevented from the necessary connection with his dad resulting in no provision of life-giving fatherly "soil" for him to take root in. Many come up against a barren, cold, and desert-like encounter as they seek for a father's masculine affirmation and identity. Some suffer actual sexual abuse, whether within one's own family or from a relative or stranger. The saddest damaging abuse would be from a father or mother, which quite often, sadly, produces examples of the abused later in life becoming abusers themselves.

A child can keep growing physically, but have his or her soul (the human *psyche*) "bonsai-ed." As he emerges into his later teens, a young man can struggle with a sense of essential ingredients missing on the inside. Some of these young men, cut off from a healthy sense of masculine identity, will see what their hearts long for in other men. They find themselves drawn to the masculine strength they see in other men and so long to be embraced and affirmed by it. It is often the 12-year-old bonsai child inside crying out for the life-giving affection and affirmation of a dad.

Other men suffering from the same lack turn to performance and become driven toward success and an endless "accumulation of trophies" in an unhealthy and addictive way. Still others turn to drugs and alcohol as an outlet for their hurt and the painful longing that they feel. There is a list of things we humans turn to in our distress. Food, sex, pornography, entertainment, and so on…

INTERNET PORN

In more recent years, it has been observed that a new emergent cause of an orientation to homosexuality is the ready availability of internet pornography. There is a lot of weird stuff out there, and a considerable amount of pornography is of a strident and erotic homosexual nature. In this way, inquisitive young men are drawn into seeing things they would never have naturally thought of themselves. They find themselves drawn in by the strong erotic nature of the images that are presented. Pornography of both heterosexual and homosexual nature (as well as a lot of other weird stuff) provides an increase of powerful psychological blocks to healthy emotional growth in sexual development and identity.

Since a lot of this happens during the time they are developing sexually, young men start connecting and relating sexually to all sorts of stuff outside of a natural relationship with a member of the opposite sex that is based on a covenant of love and respect. An orientation toward a mere fascination and obsession with sexual pleasure itself, apart from a loving relationship, can take possession of people. This may begin with simple inquisitiveness, but nonetheless any sexual pictures are extremely erotic for the male, and so he finds himself drawn into powerful experiences of sexual pleasure in ways that were never intended by the Creator.

COVENANT RELATIONSHIP—GOD'S PLAN!

Even on the more natural heterosexual level, it is damaging when sex is experienced outside of a covenant relationship and as such does not occur in the proper God-ordained context of love and trust. Where there is no relationship there can be no sense of trust and love. God intended that physical intimacy be matched with an intimacy of heart and spirit that is rooted in faithful and trustworthy covenant as a context for the creation of family and therefore community. The joy of sexual pleasure is meant to be a journey *out of* and not *into* selfishness! It is meant to be a joyful bonding agent for the delights of marriage. It is not without meaning that God chose the creation of children and thus the source of family life to be rooted in the

128

act of sexual union. Sexual union is an eternal symbol of God's power to create new life. It is chosen to be the very source of life in our world. In this sense, the act of sexual union rooted in love is to be a fountain of spontaneous joyful and beautiful (and often childlike) creativity in the context of the covenantal love and care of a shared life between a man and a woman. It is also a pathway to our destiny of becoming fathers and mothers in life. To learn how to become a father or mother in this life is part of our growing into the full image of God.

Becoming a father or mother cannot be separated from the idea of growing into the likeness of God. We are created in His image! We do not need to get married and have children in order to learn how to become mothers and fathers. You can learn to be a parent without being married—"Mother" Teresa did! It is because of this understanding that some Christian denominations have a tradition of calling their priests "Father." The path to this holy sense of Godlike parenthood and responsibility is to learn to become free from selfishness in order that we are able to pour our lives out for others. The "others" who are given to us are those who are put into our care in any way whatsoever. This includes our children, and in old age, our parents, as well as any person that falls under our authority and care at any given time. We are discipled so that we can in turn learn to bless and disciple others. In this way we grow up to become like our Father in Heaven! We are to become conduits of God's fatherly, as well as His motherly, love and care.

Something to Do

Prayerfully and with firm determination, come before God and listen to what He has to say about your sexuality. Respond with obedient faith to what He would say to you. Repent where you need to—trusting in His power and love to rescue you. Commit yourself to the journey He would take you on toward healing and holiness. Understand that healing comes from hearing Him and then freely committing yourself in faith to trust what He says and do what He asks. Ask the Father to grow you into the father or mother that He would have you become. Receive what you ask for in childlike faith. As you learn to hear and follow His Spirit, understand that it is He who will do it and that it involves a daily process of growing into all that you were created.

Chapter Fourteen

GLUE AND JELL-O

"Thou knowest that I sit waiting for the moon to turn back,
that I may listen to all the people's stories...For I am here—in
a great city—I do not obtain stories...I do merely listen,
watching for a story which I want to hear; that it may float into
my ear...I will go to sit at my home that I may listen,
turn my ears backwards to the heels of my feet on which
I wait, so that I can feel that a story is in the wind."

— Laurens van der Post, *A Story Like the Wind*.
(The prayer of a bushman who was put in prison)

He sent forth His word and healed them;
He rescued them from the grave.

—Psalm 107:19-21

A BONDING AGENT

WHEN God designed human sexuality He designed it to act like a natural bonding agent. The obvious intention is that it would be a force within marriage that would help bond a husband and wife. It is clearly the intention that intense pleasure in the act of marriage would give joy to the couple and enable them to know that they can meet each other's needs in a way that is so very personal and fulfilling! That children should be conceived at the very moment of such intimacy is also a very beautiful and holy part of the plan. That a man and a woman can partner with God in the very act of creating a child is also a clear indication that sexual intimacy should not be considered casually or flippantly.

Sexual pleasure is a very strong bonding agent. The most bonding moment occurs when orgasm is experienced. This can be very visual for the male. There is a strong tendency to bond with whatever he is looking at or focused on at the moment of orgasm. For a male it is a good thing that he should be looking into the face of the wife he loves since this will help him bond more deeply with the woman who is most precious and dear to him. If a man has spent his developing years excessively masturbating on a pornographic level, whether actually watching pornography or through his imagination, he will have bonded to a greater or lesser extent with the "things" he has been "looking at" during the experience—especially at the moment of orgasm. When such a person marries he often has varying degrees of difficulty becoming sexually aroused in the natural way that was planned by God. He has become attached and stuck (and not infrequently seriously addicted!) to something other than the natural ordained way that God had originally planned.

John's Story

John could not be aroused by his wife even after some years of marriage because of the many years of masturbating and using his imagination to "have sex" with illicit partners. Because John had been brought up in a good Christian home, the girls he would interact with in his imagination were all "bad" girls since it would not be acceptable to do this with someone who was a "good" girl—like his mother. This activity also brought with it a great deal of guilt, which in time became bonded into the whole experience.

This meant that once he was married he was not able to be sexually aroused by his "good" wife unless he imagined himself with some illicit and "bad" girl. This would help engender the feeling of guilt, which had

132

by now become part of what was needed to enable him to be aroused in order to be able to function sexually with his wife. It took much prayer and counseling to enable John to detach from what he had become bonded to so that he could begin to learn to relate to his wife as God intended and so become bonded to her in an atmosphere of real love, intimacy, and forgiveness. With God such healing and deliverance is possible. Once healed, it normally takes time and much discipline to unlearn bad habits and learn the good.

Guilt is often a significant part of what men have become bonded to because of much "illicit" sex. It is forgiveness, repentance, and then walking close to God that sets people free. It is also necessary to spend time working on what is sexually natural and good in order to develop and grow in the way God intended.

JELL-O

Another helpful way to think of the development of sexuality is to see that it is in a way like Jell-O. When you buy Jell-O in the store, it's in a powdered form. You put it into a bowl and add hot water. This dissolves and "activates" the Jell-O, transforming it into a liquid state. At first, it takes the shape of whatever container it is poured into. As time goes by it starts to set, and as it does it begins to take the shape of whatever mold it is in. Once it is solidly set, it remains in the shape of the mold even when the mold is removed. God designed our sexuality in the same way with the intention that our sexuality would conform to the particular "mold" of exclusive covenant relationship and intimate love shared in the context of a particular marriage between a man and a woman.

When sexuality is initially aroused during adolescence, it goes from the powder to the "liquid" state in which it can take the shape of just about anything it is poured into! If that "container" happens to be pornography, some other perversion, or simply "forbidden fruit" with its accompanying sense of shame and guilt, it begins to "take the shape" of those things. Frequently a sense of guilt is included in the mix. Over a period of time, the means of sexual arousal takes the shape of this wrong mold and then, after it sets, struggles and finds it nearly impossible to change to the normal, natural, and beautiful ways that were lovingly thought up by the Creator. Dr Weis, a man who counsels people with sexual problems, tells of a the story of a particular man who needed to have his boots on in order to make love to his wife—prior to his marriage he had habitually masturbated standing up and looking down at his boots! Weird but true!

Some Things to Do

Thank God that He is able to forgive and heal all who come to Him for help. He has promised this! Healing and deliverance always begin at the cross where sins are confessed and forgiven. This is the first step. The second step, which is most essential, is that we come to terms with the Lordship of Christ. That is, we need to acknowledge His way rather than ours. Then, with the promised power and help of the Holy Spirit, we move on in faith to learn to listen for His loving voice and obey all He says to us in regard to all things—including our sexuality! It is only as we go on in intimate relationship with Him that we are ultimately healed and set free. There are all sorts of good programs and methods that can help up to a point. It is, however, a daily living by faith in the loving and healing presence of God that is ultimately going to do it! There is no shortcut around that. That God and His children should be forever one was the original intent of creation!

Spend time with God prayerfully considering His love for you.

Come to terms with and freely submit to the Lordship of Christ in your life and over your sexuality.

Ask in faith, never doubting, that the Holy Spirit can and will open your eyes and set you free.

Learn to listen daily for the voice of Jesus and follow Him in the new ways in which He would lead you. Bear in mind He will be leading you out of the guilt and *secrecy* of any addiction, therefore do not be too surprised that the path may not be easy. Trust Him, He will not harm you. Do not shrink back in pain, humiliation, or despair. He will heal you, and the healing effect on others will be unimaginable!

Chapter Fifteen

HEALING FOR WOMEN

"He sent forth His word and healed them..."

—Psalm 107:20

"As a mother comforts her child, so will I comfort you; and you will be comforted over Jerusalem. When you see this, your heart will rejoice and you will flourish like grass..."

—Isaiah 66:13-14

MOTHERS

BOTH small boys and girls need to be caressed often with tender kindness and gentle words of affectionate affirmation. A crucial need for gender development, particularly in a girl in her early years of life, is that she receives affection and a sense of acceptance and warmth from her mother. To hear, "You are my sweetheart...you are Mommy's little angel...you are so beautiful...you are adorable and lovable..." and so on, is imperative for her to be able to receive a sense of confident and joyful feminine identity. Mothers can impart a sense of feminine identity and beauty to little girls in a way that no one else can. Little girls are crying out, "Please tell me who I am," and it is a mother saying, "You're loveable, you are mommy's angel, you are mommy's pretty little girl" that does so much good work in establishing a positive, secure, and peaceful feminine identity.

A woman who struggles with being in touch with her own sense of God-given inner beauty and loveliness lacks the ability to properly nurture her own children in these important ways. Perhaps she expresses love in only practical ways or just out of a sense of duty because this is all she can do as she too is struggling with her own hurts and a lack of feeling nurtured and loved. One cannot give what one has not received! Little girls can grow up with a sense of emptiness and deep longing from a lack of a mother's affection and affirmation and so may not feel that they are beautiful, loveable, or precious.

In her teenage years, such a young woman may begin to see what she longs for in another woman. She sees the other woman as loveable and beautiful and possessing all the qualities that she feels she does not have. In this way, she may well find herself powerfully drawn to someone of her own sex in order to receive the feminine love and affirmation she hungers for.[1] Some grow this way because they have grown up with "barren soil" in their developmental root system. As fallen and broken creatures we lack more than we could sometimes imagine when it comes to loving each other, and in particular our children. We are all in need of much grace and help from the Father. His promise is that if we ask we receive, if we seek we find, and if we knock the door will open for us.

A FATHER'S ROLE

A father also plays an important role in communicating a sense of love and beauty to little girls, but he cannot substitute for the work that only a mother can do—especially during the early developmental years of life. The father's work in the matter of imparting good feminine identity becomes more important as the girl reaches her teens. At that stage a young woman needs a father to speak to and treat her with respect, a sense of delight, and gentle loving protection. He needs to express joy in her being beautiful and lovable. For a father not to be overbearing and controlling is an art to be learned. When a father has been absent or unavailable to his daughter, or even hurtful and offensive, healing only comes when she forgives her father and with the subsequent and imperative obedience to the healing and life-giving whisperings of love that flow from the heart of God. He alone is able to heal and lovingly restore.

Another significant cause of an orientation toward lesbianism can occur when a young girl is abused by a member of the opposite sex. The horror and fear of the abuse can cause a little girl to recoil from or reject her feminine identity and her sexuality. Abused girls can come to feel that being a girl is a bad thing. Often they feel dirty. Nonetheless, deep in their hearts they still long for feminine identity: to know who they are and what it means to be a woman. For this reason, some find themselves seeking this affirmation from another woman. Jesus can heal wounds. There is no condemnation in Him. He is full of amazing love and grace and an unimaginable desire to lift, heal, save, and redeem.

There can be many different types of rocky and barren soil in our root systems—experiences that stop us from growing into what God created us to be. Wounds received can drive different temperament types in different directions. One young person, because he doesn't receive love—or perhaps the wrong kind of love—from his parents, can choose to receive value and identity from performance. This can grow into living life out of a drivenness toward success and a hunger for power. Such a man or woman doesn't feel real or whole inside so they addictively run after power and success, which can, like a drug, make them feel temporarily and sporadically better about themselves. They can end up surrounding themselves with symbols of success to try to make their lives meaningful and significant. It doesn't work long-term. All these things, like drugs, give you a high for a little while, but then drop you. The next time around there is a craving for more. The high is never quite as high again, and the lows continue to get lower.

Other personality types cannot quite manage the rat race and its drive for success and end up falling into depression, despondency, and a sense of failure. They feel immobilized and hopeless. Such people can end up addicted to drugs and alcohol to ease the pain and hurt. A lack of good nurturing and a healthy impartation of a sense of significant identity from a mother and father can lead to a sense of lack and in some cases even neuroses. People turn to alcohol, drugs, sex, shopping, entertainment, or overeating for comfort and escape. The list of possibilities is long. Still others move toward performance as they seek identity and value and bury themselves in their work in an unhealthy but seemingly productive way. This describes the classic picture of a father who brings home a large paycheck thinking that he has done what is needed. While he feels successful in doing his duty, his wife and children may be starving for love, friendship, and intimacy.

Some of these neurotic and compulsive habits are actually praised and valued by our culture! The young woman who thought she ought to spend inordinate hours in fretful prayer "passionately" seeking God in order to please Him was no doubt seen by many as being wonderfully spiritual and good and hailed as an excellent example to her peers. When such neurotic behavior is praised by well-meaning friends and authority figures, it is reinforced. There is a place for passionate and even desperate prayer, but not the kind that is neurotic and out of touch with the senses of inner peace, quiet confidence, and rest in the love, faithfulness, and goodness of God.

I remember a little girl in a Christian community who was overly kind and helpful. Most everyone praised her as she continued to serve people around her in so many ways. It took a perceptive and kind friend of mine to call attention to her compliant behavior as being "overboard," an aberration that needed correcting. If left unnoticed, she may have become an easy target for those who would have manipulated her into doing whatever *they* wanted.

So much in our lives goes back to our relationship with parents, siblings, schoolteachers, coaches, etc. Even well-meaning pastors and church leaders can unwittingly hurt us by encouraging and reinforcing things we need to be freed from. Parents can hurt their children and not even know they are doing it. As with the anorexic, often the parents do not realize they are being overbearing and controlling. They are simply encouraging their kids toward greater achievement and success. Some comply in an unhealthy way and run after a compulsive, competitive drive for perfection.

Some quite "demented" men and women in our society are hailed in the media as superheroes. They are recognized as great performers and successful people. Many have become rich and famous. Money, popularity, and recognition are the all-too-common means we use to fix the broken image we have of ourselves. God wants to heal us and set us free to know who we are in His eyes. Are we loved children, or have we become orphans who must frantically fend for ourselves?

I am not suggesting that we not encourage our children to do well or not praise them when they do. Of course, they need affirmation and encouragement, but not as the primary way to value them. As with so many things in life it is a question of wisdom and balance. Too little food can kill a person as easily as too much! The truth that sets us free is almost always a question of balance. Truth is more often a question of "both and" rather than "either or."

SOMETHING TO DO

Quietly listen to the Father. Hear what the Spirit would say to you regarding the things in this chapter.

Present yourself to Him as a living sacrifice, asking that the Father would help you know the ways you need to be freed from the patterns of this world. Repent and trust Him as He leads you. By faith receive His enabling love and power.

Ask Him to show you His good, pleasing, and perfect will and way in your life. Trust Him to work in you to make you willing and able to respond to His love and obey Him.

ENDNOTE

1. Other women can seek identity in performance or in the pursuit of men for the same reasons. The different choices are often determined by having different dispositions and temperaments.

Chapter Sixteen

In Pursuit of Identity

"What springs from my self and not from God is evil:
It is a perversion of something of God's.
Whatever is not of faith is sin; it is a stream cut off –
a stream that cuts itself off from its source
and thinks to run on without it."

—George MacDonald,
Unspoken Sermons—The Inheritance

COOLNESS AND THE PURSUIT OF IDENTITY

NOT very long ago, in the jungles of Papua New Guinea, people went about naked. Well, not quite! The men would wear a gourd—it was a long, thin hollowed out type of pumpkin skin. This inordinately long item, in some cases two to three feet long, was worn over the penis and was held up (in an "erect" position) by a thong around the neck—a new twist on "clothes make the man!"

Down through the ages the penis has been a symbol of man's manhood and virility. In Papua the gourd was a way to draw attention to the importance and station of a man. The picture of the jungle man proudly wearing his giant gourd tells a straightforward and honest story of what fallen men seek to do everywhere. They walk around with this attachment as if to say, "Look how big and important I am," while underneath there hides a much smaller and less confident truth. This style of dress is, in Western eyes, primitive—and embarrassing for the missionaries who go there! But in the modern Western world, men do the same thing, simply in more sophisticated ways. And yes—even in the church! The world is full of anxious and hurt people who feel quite small and broken deep down inside, and so they strive, using their own gifts and resources, to create the illusion that they are somehow bigger, stronger, and more successful than they really are. We spend a large part of our lives determinedly maneuvering to create some very impressive gourds, yet unaware of the illusion.

There are countless examples of these gourds, from the simple and obvious to the complex and more subtle. Even the simple and obvious gourds *can* still be impressively large, powerful, and expensive—luxury cars, large and imposing SUVs, or rough and tough pickup trucks with a gun rack to boot. And maybe the most modern phallic symbol of all, a powerful, loud, throbbing Harley motorcycle between one's legs! Beyond these are multimillion-dollar yachts and jets for those able to achieve the most extravagant levels.

Adorning one's body with expensive clothes and jewelry is a more direct imitation of wearing a gourd, as is developing one's body with endless hours in the gym to project the proper image. If that's too much work, one can go through the passive pain of enduring many tattoos to make a different or additional statement about one's body. One can also "wear" an important job and an important-sounding job title and of course one can combine any number of these for a synergistic effect! In any of these areas, bigger or smaller seems to be an indication of one's station in life. Along with these quite obvious gourds, there are the more subtle gourds evidenced by the various intellectual brands of fame pursued in the arts, music, and academia, and some highly intellectual and skilled professions. For others there is also the possibility of becoming one of the superheroes in the world of sports. Where I live, there are men (and even some women) who walk or "strut" in a way that sets them apart. And there are countless "cool" and unique ways to talk.

After exposing these things, you may now find it hard to believe that there is nothing inherently wrong with many if not all of the material gifts listed above, especially if we do not think of them in terms of "my" or "mine." Nor is there anything inherently wrong with dressing well, exercising regularly, striving to attain the most challenging and fulfilling job for your abilities, striving for excellence in that job, or continually studying and improving your intellectual capacity. It's just that we are so often seriously out of balance. We have let these things define us and we worship them. There is something deep in the hearts of striving people crying out, "Who am I? Please tell me who I am—tell me I am somebody—tell me I am loved and that I have value." This need must be answered and satisfied before one could ever hope to keep these other things in balance.

THE POWER OF THE CROSS

So much of our anxious striving is false and needs to be recognized and confessed as sin. The power that is able to destroy and remove the obstacles that get in the way of becoming real is the power of forgiveness. The central significance of the cross is that it is the place where God forgave—and forgives—the sins of the world. Through what Jesus did on the cross, we are forgiven and we are able to forgive ourselves and others. This is the beginning of God's way for us. The blood of Jesus is the power by which we are enabled to forgive ourselves of all the bad stuff that we have done and also to forgive others for what has been done to us. When forgiveness has done its work, then all sin loses its power and can no longer hold us prisoners. We can move on to the real life for which we were created, an eternal journey of relationship with the Father.

POWER TO DEFEAT DEMONS

Some years ago in South Africa I was trying to cast a demon out of a white woman who had been raped, on two different occasions, by black men. The experiences of being raped had opened her heart to a demonic spirit of resentment and hatred toward black men. It was a type of demon that manifested itself by taking over control of the personality and speaking through the victim. We confronted the demon in the name of Jesus, but we could not get the demon to leave. The demon would simply say, "I have a right to be here and you cannot chase me out of this woman…she is mine!" We resorted to shouting louder, but it didn't help. Somehow we lacked authority to expel the demon.

Eventually we decided we should ask Jesus to tell us what to do. Good move! We needed a gift of discernment from the Spirit to know what was going on and what to do. The Holy Spirit spoke to us telling us that the woman must first go to the cross and forgive the men who raped her. True forgiveness in the name of Jesus is the only thing that will destroy the power of sin and evil and free us from demons that enslave. True repentance and faith in the blood of Christ to grant forgiveness brings healing and deliverance.

She agreed with us that the blood of Jesus was shed to forgive the men who had hurt her so deeply. We helped her prayerfully hand them over to Jesus. It was now time to pray against the demon. As I started to address the demon I thought there would be another struggle as before. I barely said, "In the Name of Jesus, be gone," and the demon left instantly with an expulsion of air from the woman's mouth. There was no more struggle. The demon had lost its power and could no longer resist. The careful, Holy Spirit-led appropriation of the blood of Jesus in her life won the battle and gave us easy authority over the enemy where we had none before! Appropriating the forgiveness that comes to us through the cross (as the Holy Spirit leads) is vital to our deliverance from sin and the powers of evil.

Demonic strongholds are in the mind. This woman had allowed a belief system of hatred toward black men to develop and that gave an opening to the controlling power of the enemy spirit. The enemy had been given a reason to be there. The work of faith in prayerfully expressing forgiveness through the cross of Jesus destroyed the hard "rocks" that had been dramatically put in place as an obstacle to her growth many years before. She was set free through the forgiveness that flows from the cross, and she began to allow herself to be rooted in the love of God.

The only thing that will ultimately heal and deliver people is a real, living encounter with God. There is no scientific or technical method that can give life and heal. There are many good and important principles that we can respond to, but in the final analysis it is only the presence of God that will ultimately save us. There is no shortcut around an encounter with the living God of love. We are to hear and respond to what He would say. When we repent and deal with forgiveness as His Spirit leads us, we are healed and set free.

A JOURNEY

Deliverance and healing is also a journey. It begins with—but does not end with—forgiveness. In the name of Jesus you must forgive anyone (including yourself) who has hurt you or owes you. It does not matter what it is or how bad it is. Take it to the cross, the place of forgiveness, and put it all under the blood of Jesus. We must do this and do it thoroughly! In your imagination see it happening—see the cross—see all the sin and hurt going into Jesus on the cross. See the blood of Jesus washing it away. Receive it by faith and take it into your heart. Forgiveness is the deepest way of receiving and giving love. This is the first and most vital step.

After the appropriation of forgiveness we begin a disciplined journey of walking with Him in the power of the Holy Spirit. We receive a righteousness that comes directly from Him, is revealed to us, and is appropriated by faith alone. It is a journey in which we learn to live by faith as children of the Eternal Father. Jesus told us that He knew His sheep, and they would listen for His voice and follow Him! We are to learn to live in a real relationship with Him in which we hear and follow His voice.

It is faith alone that pleases God. We are, with the help of the Spirit, to develop a childlike trust in His love and His promise to empower us to hear and follow Him. Peter imagined that in himself he could be faithful to Jesus while the others forsook Him. For this reason, satan was permitted to test Peter, but only to the extent that the notion that he had what it took to follow Jesus would be swept away and that faith and faith alone would remain. In the end Peter was told that one day he would be faithful to death. The difference is that Jesus was now the one who was saying it. Peter's response was simply to believe Jesus with a faith refined by fire! His confession became,

"Lord, You know all things…You know that I love you" (John 21:17). After the awful test it was uncomplicated childlike faith in Jesus and not in himself that remained. The lie of thinking he had it within himself to follow Jesus was forever gone. Peter was then given the commission to strengthen his brothers, *"Feed My sheep…"* (see John 21:17).

It is only when we are stripped down to naked childlike faith that we are best able to strengthen and help our brothers and sisters. It is in our weakness that true strength can be perfected.

> *Simon, Simon, Satan has asked to sift you as wheat. But I have prayed for you, Simon, that your faith may not fail. And when you have turned back, strengthen your brothers* (Luke 22:31-32).

Something to Do

Paul said that he had discovered a secret—that the real strength of God was discovered only when he realized his own weakness.

> *But he said to me, "My grace is sufficient for you, for my power is made perfect in weakness." Therefore I will boast all the more gladly about my weaknesses, so that Christ's power may rest on me. That is why, for Christ's sake, I delight in weaknesses, in insults, in hardships, in persecutions, in difficulties. For when I am weak, then I am strong* (2 Corinthians 12:9-11).

Ask God to show you what needs to be stripped away from you in order that you might find your real true self—the child that God loves and would drench with real and eternal love, power, and joy.

148

Chapter Seventeen

MISOGYNY AND CHAUVINISM

God's power differs from powerlessness, is superior to the other
powers, is victoriously opposed to "power in itself," in being
the power of law, i.e. of His love activated and revealed in Jesus
Christ and thus the content, the determination and the limit of
everything possible, and the power over and in all that is real.

—Karl Barth, *Dogmatics in Outline*

God's power is the fabric of existence.

—Zellyn James Hunter

"I should like balls infinitely better," she replied, "if they
were carried on in a different manner; but there is something
insufferably tedious in the usual process of such a meeting. It
would surely be much more rational if conversation instead of
dancing made the order of the day."
"Much more rational, my dear Caroline, I dare say, but it would
not be near so much like a ball."

—Jane Austen, *Pride and Prejudice*

BIBLE scholars have through the centuries thought that God's creation of Adam, the man, is a symbol of the Creator and that Eve, as
a woman, is a symbol of the creature, or of all that is creaturely. It

is of course quite obvious that the man is himself a mere creature and as such is completely equal to the woman. As fellow creatures, both of them together are the "Bride of Christ."

Lucifer too, is a created being. We are given to understand that he was a quite magnificent angel and something of a worship leader in Heaven. As a "creature" he is depicted by Michelangelo in the Sistine Chapel in female form. Here, in the eye of the artist, he appears in a symbolic way with a female torso with the tail of a serpent—I suppose something like a "snake-maid" rather than a mermaid. C.S. Lewis also depicts the enemy as the female White Witch in *The Chronicles of Narnia*, the "creature" in rebellion against the creator of Narnia. This is absolutely not meant to reflect on women as being in any way more evil than men. Certainly not! It is done simply with the understanding that the female form is, in a significant way, an appropriate symbol of all that is creaturely. This of course includes all men! In this regard, Paul tells us that "in Christ" there is neither male nor female.

When lucifer in his rebellion rejected being under the authority of the Creator, he decided that he would be the master of his own destiny. He would be "god" for himself. He would be his own highest authority. He would presume to fill himself from his own emptiness. We, in turn, rejected our created emptiness and our need to be filled in favor of the illusion that we can fill ourselves. It is as if an eye were to say to the sun, "I have no need of you. I can make my own light;" or if an ear were to say to sound, "I do not need you; I can be sound and speech for myself;" or if lungs were to say to the air, "I have no need of you; I can produce my own oxygen." The thought, "I can define myself and determine my own destiny without any help from above" is like a book saying at some point in its writing, "I will become my own author." The grasp for independence and the shutting out of God's love and authority is the essence of evil. It is both the essence and cause of our fallen-ness.

In the quote from *Pride and Prejudice* at the beginning of this chapter, Caroline Bingley displays a rejection of dancing as a means of social interaction and relationship in favor of rational conversation. The more "feminine" art of dancing is rejected as inferior to the more superior "masculine" work of rational conversation. In our fallen natures there is too often an elevation of the technical approach that gives ready power and a tendency to relegate to a position of less importance the artful, responsive, and mysterious ways of the heart (intuition). Misogyny, the overt and strident kinds and the more subtle and patronizing kinds, is born from this tendency.

Misogyny is the hatred of women. It is also, in a spiritual sense, the hatred and rejection of all that is "feminine" in God's creation. The rejection of a responsive, childlike trust in God in preference of independent and grasping self-determination is an act of misogyny and as such is at the very heart and nature of evil. It is the beginning and root of all sin. It is a lie... and the "father" of all successive lies.

Satan rejected the idea of responding to and trusting the Creator and grasped at being his own master and source of life and destiny. This rejection of being a creature, responsive to the Creator, is also, in essence, a rejection of all that is characteristically feminine. It is a refusal to receive from the Father the love and direction He would pour out. On the level of human physiology, it is as if the female were to say to the male, "I have no need of you. I can bear life on my own," as if the empty space within the female could fill itself.

In this sense satan's rebellion is misogynistic to the very core. It is an outright rejection and hatred of all that is creaturely, and therefore feminine, and able to respond. As I say these things, do not forget that both men and women are creatures and therefore predominantly "feminine" in relation to the Creator. The Church is, for this reason, referred to in Scripture as the Bride of Christ. Through the Fall, both Adam and Eve, in the end, lose their sense of the true feminine and also, therefore, their sense of the true masculine. The true masculine is replaced by an ersatz, chauvinistic, insecure, and dominating counterfeit and the true feminine is replaced, on the one hand, by a false manipulative control, and on the other hand, by a subservient pathetic compliancy. Both men and women can express either the false masculine or the false feminine nature within their respective genders.

It is important to note that manipulation can stem from a sense of weakness and pathetic helplessness. In some cases this broken feminine image invites and welcomes the broken masculine image of superiority and domination. These can be found in either gender. Unfortunately, these fallen, broken, and false images of masculinity and femininity are often taught in church as right, acceptable, and even biblical. There can also be a false kind of masculinity that asserts its power or control in the form of stubborn legless withdrawal and abdication into silence and passivity. The broken and fallen parts of man have many faces—that is, many sides.

In the Garden of Eden satan tempted mankind, represented by Adam and Eve, into repeating, in essence, what he himself had done. The temptation was for the man and woman to reject their responsive trust of and submission to the Creator and to choose independence and self-determination. To reach for the fruit of the tree of the knowledge of good and evil was to become wise "like God," knowing good and evil—by means of acquiring knowledge. Imagine the enemy suggesting that there was a way in which we, on our own, could become more like Jesus! This was the invitation: to be more like God, to grow up. The deception was that we could achieve it ourselves.

From a symbolic point of view it is significant that the serpent's strike was initially against Eve, the feminine component of humankind. If he could just get that part of God's image, the woman, the primary symbol of all that is responsive in creation, to withdraw in independence from trusting the loving initiative of Heaven, it would result in separation and death. Satan would have them in the grasp of his suffocating coils. At the heart of our fallen-ness lies a misogynistic rejection of our femininity (our "creaturely-ness") and the acceptance of a false masculinity (our own "godness"), which results in our desire to have exclusive authorship over our own lives and destinies.

Evil frequently has as a cardinal characteristic an inherent drive to reject weakness and grasp for power. This was the enemy's temptation to Adam and Eve in the Garden. It was to reject all that was feminine in themselves and grasp for "godlike" masculine power on the basis of the rational but horribly mistaken use of knowledge. Adam and Eve chose to trust a rational and, I dare say, theological formula as the means of harnessing the power to achieve the goal of "becoming." Apparently it would make them wiser and more like God. Whatever could be wrong with that? They of course learned that knowledge alone had no power to give life. This misuse of knowledge merely brought separation from the Father who had created and loved them. It left them desolate and alone with a mysterious new awareness that they were naked—a stream cut off from its source!

Since the Fall, life on our planet has been plagued by the curse of an overriding misogyny which began in the Garden. There is in our fallen nature a preference for things masculine over things feminine. This is done by both men and women. Misogyny can even express itself through feminism of all things! Some feminism wages a ruthless war against and rejects much of which is truly and beautifully feminine in order to make women "equal" with men. This type of feminism is oddly macho and chauvinistic—a strident ersatz masculinity dressed in drag!

Whether it be the superiority of men over women, science and technology over art, thinking over feeling, discursive reason over imagination, or Western culture with its emphasis on productivity and technology over African and Eastern cultures with their emphasis on intuition, art, music, and relationships, there is no doubt that one is more frequently seen as superior to the other.

The preference of things masculine over things feminine is very obvious within our modern Western educational systems. For the most part, technical and practical skills are valued. Creative, intuitive thinking is played down and often considered insignificant. Although misogyny does not always win, consider what the world's loss might have been had it won in the following men's lives: A young Einstein was told by his Professor in the science department that he would never make a scientist because he did not think or behave like one. The ingenious and creative Winston Churchill was kept back at school since he failed a year. C.S. Lewis got into Oxford as a student only because of a special dispensation to accept men coming home from the war in Europe. His math was not up to standard!

One morning I found an essay that my youngest son had written while attending high school in North Georgia in the United States. It was quite well written and I was especially impressed by his creativity and imagination.

When he came home I told him how impressed I was. With a sad cynicism he told me that everything I had praised about his essay meant nothing at school. The teachers, in his opinion, would not even know what I was talking about. He informed me that he would only be graded on certain points. There must be an opening paragraph, three points, a closing paragraph, and the grammar and punctuation must be correct. The message of the essay, no matter how creative, would not count or even be noticed. How sad.

Modern educational policy with its, in some cases, almost exclusive slant toward productivity is also serving to discourage a great deal of creative aptitude in many young people. The creative thinkers who survive the system will have to be quite courageous. Sometimes even the strong intuitive thinkers emerge scarred and wounded in the face of so much dull mechanical opposition. Thank God some manage to get by. Many other more "right-brained" young people go through life believing the subtle message they have been told: that they are inferior and of less value than their more "productive" brothers and sisters. This too is a subtle expression of the misogyny that came into our world with the Fall.

Consider the following letter I recently received from one of my students. There are many like him.

> Hi Angus,
>
> I wanted to pass along to you a great testimony of what God is doing in my life. Ever since I met with you, God has been doing amazing things in restoring my "right-brained-ness" and reviving my creative juices. I don't know if you remember, but when we met, you told me that I was an "artist" rather than a "cowboy" and that this didn't mean that I was any less of a man. I think that (in my ignorance) I was offended to be called an artist, but since then, God has been exposing this truth in my life. When I was a young boy—particularly growing up in South America—I used to be constantly complemented by parents, teachers, and friends for my creativity. I used to love to draw, paint, and play musical instruments. I was a huge fan of science fiction

and I loved the outdoors. However, since I moved to North America, I think that the desire to succeed, especially in school, really quenched all of this. I became really good at memorizing and at doing all the things that enabled me to get good grades in school. I eventually gravitated toward the business field in late high school and college and really excelled in this area. I began to read lots of business books and became really good at business writing. Funny thing, when I applied to graduate business school, I had to take a standardized graduate school admission test. Part of the test is to write an essay, which, for the first time, was being graded by a computer! Guess what; I got a perfect grade on my essay! I had perfect structure; placing all the transition sentences at the right points with well formulated opening and closing paragraphs. Never mind what I actually wrote—it could have been completely incomprehensible! Anyway, the past few years, by the grace of God, I have begun to embrace the artist in me. I have fallen in love with nature again! I am actually reading science fiction books and am loving them! I feel like a little boy because I can't wait to get home from work and read the next page! I have picked up and started playing musical instruments and there's a hunger in me to start drawing. It's such an exciting feeling, Gus. I feel like I'm myself again. I feel like something inside of me that was dead for so long is being revived! I feel so much less insecure about myself—like I've re-discovered my identity. I'm so full of joy and enjoyment of life. I just felt like I had to share this with you—partly because of the influence that you had in it, and also because I know that you would understand. It's like what C.S. Lewis says, that our enjoyment of something is "consummated" by telling someone else about it. I just love hearing you teach, Gus. It brings life to my soul. Last night I went home so excited and full of joy, knowing that there's hope for people like me! Listening to you helps me to get in touch with the artist inside of me and it is such a great feeling! Thanks Gus, for speaking the truth into my life and helping me to re-gain my identity! You know, I think that had I not come here to Texas and gone through what I did, I would have continued to excel in the business world. I'm sure I would have made lots of money and had a successful career. But I would have gone through life being someone that I was not made to be! What a shock this is to me. I am so thankful that the Lord chose to rescue me from an empty way of life!

Blessings,
Peter

GOD'S REDEMPTIVE WAYS

In the story of the coming of the Messiah to our world, Mary's part in the redemption drama indicates the height of honor to which God raises the place of woman in her very special and unique ability to respond to life and obey the call and initiative of Heaven. A young girl with her special God-given qualities is the means by which the Kingdom of Heaven comes to earth! It is only as we follow the example of trust and response set for us by Mary that this world is redeemed! In this she is our pattern, a true mother and good teacher to us all. She is there to influence and show us the way—to follow Jesus. The story of Mary is a heavenly affirmation of all that is able to respond in humans and therefore bring redemption into the world. "Be it unto me according to your word for I am the handmaiden of the Lord." It is not by our attempts at "powerful" works of righteousness that we are saved but by the childlike faith and obedient response to a loving and merciful God. He comes to fill us with His resplendent presence and overflowing life, and we are empty no longer!

At the Second Vatican Council called by Pope John XXIII, the unpredictable and enigmatic Assembly of God pastor, David du Plessis, was asked by a Catholic priest what he thought of Mary. David answered wisely that he was a faithful and obedient disciple of Mary. He went on to explain that Mary gave only one command in the Scripture. It was at the wedding in Cana when she pointed to Jesus and instructed the servants with a firm and confident, "Do whatever He tells you." In this, Mary, as a woman created in the image of God, is a wonderful symbol of all that is truly and beautifully feminine in creation. All true men and women are called by the Father, like Mary, to point the world to Jesus with the call to "do whatever He tells you!"

Our true initiative and action is born out of our God-given ability to respond to the realities of Heaven. In the face of the call of the Prince of Heaven to obedience and discipleship, both men and women are equal before God. As we listen in quiet submission, all that is truly creaturely and feminine in us is called forth in both men and women. As we obey, all that is truly lordly and masculine is called forth in both men and women. As we learn to trust (respond) and obey (initiate), redeemed men learn what it means to be the Bride of Christ and redeemed women learn how to become sons of God. In the spiritual sense, there is a true "Mary" in every man and a potential warrior and son (a Joan of Arc) in every woman. Of course, we would be most accurate to say there is a true reflection and expression of Jesus in every man and woman alike, realizing that it is not His physical gender that indwells us, but, through the Holy Spirit, it is His feminine response and masculine obedience that indwells and operates through us! Authority and submission. The whole and complete image of God is thus perfected in both men and women as they behold what manner of love the Father has bestowed upon them that they should be called sons of God! Lamb and Lion! In the image of God. Hallelujah! Holy, Holy, Holy... Heaven and earth are full of Your glory! Hosanna in the highest!

What to Do...

*Repent and believe and you shall be saved...*Pause and think about what God is saying to you about this.

- Spend some time asking God to give you revelation concerning the ways in which you have been misogynistic and independent. Do this not just on a physical level but also on a psychological (soul) and spiritual level.

- Prayerfully ask the Holy Spirit to reveal to you the manner in which you should repent and respond to Jesus and the Father. Do it!

- Ask God to reveal to you what thoughts and ideas should replace the ones you are repenting from. See yourself embracing and taking in what He shows you. Let the Holy Spirit renew your mind so that you would know God's good, pleasing, and perfect will.

- Ask God to fill you with the Holy Spirit and empower you to hear His voice, then follow Him believing that "For in the Gospel a righteousness which God ascribes is revealed, both springing from faith and leading to faith [disclosed through the way of faith that arouses to more faith]…" (Rom. 1:17 AMP).

- Prayerfully commit yourself to fully trust that He will lead you by His Spirit so that like Jesus, whom you are called to follow, you would do only what you see the Father doing: "Jesus gave them this answer: 'I tell you the truth, the Son can do nothing by Himself; He can do only what He sees His Father doing, because whatever the Father does the Son also does'" (John 5:19).

Thank Him—by faith—for His faithfulness and that He will answer your prayer!

The above needs to be done on a daily basis until it becomes part of the fabric of who you are. In this way we learn to practice the Presence of God.

THE MISSION

"...continue to work out your salvation with fear and trembling, for it is God who works in you to will and to act according to His good purpose."

—Philippians 2:12-13

"There was a towering desire within him to reveal his Father in serving the poor, the captive, the blind, and all who are in need. Jesus was entirely devoured by his mission. It was the experience of the Father's holiness that created the imperative of preaching the reign of God's justice, peace, and forgiving love."

—Brennan Manning, *Reflections for Ragamuffins*

GOD, who is love, wants to reverse what happened at the Fall, and He wants to begin to do it now! He wants to restore His broken image. It is for this reason that Christ died and He sent His Spirit. It is Christ in us the hope of glory—and glory is reaching our full potential in Christ. We are to be one with Him...even as He and the Father are one. This is the purpose of life and the goal of redemption. It is not that we should be good. Impossible! There is none good—only God. It is that He who is goodness should live in us and through us. We are to be Jesus to the world. That is the Gospel. Christ, living in you!

> *I have been crucified with Christ and I no longer live, but Christ lives in me. The life I live in the body, I live by faith in the Son of God, who loved me and gave Himself for me* (Galatians 2:20).

First, by faith we reckon our old self to be dead—crucified with Christ. Oh, but I am not dead—I am alive!—Oh, but it is Christ now who lives in me...His Spirit and my spirit have become one...and the life of the new me, I live by faith in the Son of God. We are no longer under the law but alive to the Spirit. For as many as are led by the Spirit are the sons of God!

In the Garden of Eden, humanity shut God out by choosing from free will to live from the inherent power of the gifts of their own souls rather than live from a relationship with the eternal Father. Whether we live from the "bad" side of knowledge or, like Job and Saul (before he became Paul), from the "good" side of knowledge, we are in sin. Independence is the essence of sin. Paul, who said he was "faultless" before the law also claimed to be the chief of sinners. Trying to be good without Him is the worst kind of sin. We cannot do anything about our fallen nature; we need Jesus to rescue us from the quagmire of ourselves so that He, who is righteousness, can live in us. Any attempt to do it ourselves or improve ourselves by our own effort is not what He wants or what we were created for. We are to live by faith. *"Without faith it is impossible to please God"* (Heb. 11:6).

The salvation we are to work out each day is that it is *God* who is at work in us to make us both willing and able to obey His purpose. His purpose is that we should be indwelt by His Presence and listen for His voice and follow Him. The Scriptures tell us that all who are led by the Spirit are sons of God! (see Rom. 8:14). He is the Power and the Love we need.

Without Him, we can do nothing. We are negative and He is positive. Only as I am filled each moment by His positive Presence, and therefore His goodness, do I become positive and thereby filled with Him who is Righteousness and Holiness.

A great recurring error in the world (and often in the church) is that we think of righteousness and holiness as if they are something that is separate from the person of God. We think they are something we can achieve, no doubt with His help. Nonsense! We do this because we feel (in our soul) separated from Him, and so we separate morality and the law from Him. This is the very thing that causes us to live out of stress and anxiety and not out of trust and rest. God is not righteous; He is Righteousness! God is not good; He is Goodness. God does not obey the law of love; He is Love. Apart from Him these things do not exist, and any idea of them existing apart from Him is the great illusion we get from having eaten from the tree of knowledge! Ultimately, the law is not something God obeys as if it is something apart from Him and to which He submits. If this were so, He would not be God!

The law is, ultimately, how things work. The universe works in and from God who is Love. It has its existence in Him and from Him. Nothing exists apart from God and He is Love. In Him we move and have our being.

He is our Righteousness! He is Holiness, He is Goodness, and He is Love, Peace, and Joy. Any self-righteousness, self love, or self good is negative—empty—an illusion that ultimately causes stress and anxious thinking, or whatever the opposite of rest and true peace is. He alone is all in all. He is El Shaddai, Almighty God, the All Sufficient in whom all things exist and are held together.

The Gospel is Jesus and Jesus is the Gospel. It is not something we tell people about Him. People do not know the Gospel until they know Jesus. The Gospel is not some abstraction about Him. It is Him! In John chapter 3, we are told that when we are "born again" we *see* the Kingdom of God. He is the Kingdom—it does not exist as something apart from Him. In Heaven light is not something…it is Someone. The Bible tells us this plainly.

The whole plan of redemption is headed for a great marriage feast in which all things will be restored to their proper place—in Him. Christ is the head. Christ in all things and all things being one in Christ. This is the purpose of creation. All creation waits on tiptoe for the sons of God to arise. The sons of God are the Bride of Christ who has become one with Him.

They are men and women who have come, by faith, to be filled with Jesus. We are all Jesus with different flavors. The following song puts it well:

> I am covered over with a robe of righteousness
> which Jesus gives to me.
>
> I am covered over with the precious blood of Jesus
> and He lives in me.
>
> What a joy it is to know my Heavenly Father loves me so
> and gives to me—my Jesus.
>
> When He looks at me He sees not what I used to be
> but He sees Jesus.

He is the great and only Initiator of all life. We respond by faith, are filled, and are no longer empty. Hallelujah! The Spirit becomes a spring of living water within us welling up to eternal life. It is all Jesus…and we are complete only in Him. All this is only possible by faith and faith alone. This is who we are, our true and real identity.

Each of us is a unique expression of Him for His glory. Glory simply means reaching our full potential in Him…being one with Him. Glory is Him in us. Christ in me the hope of glory! No more, no less. He is in us and we are in Him! We are filled with the divine Love by which the universe is held together and works. Any choice, either from the good side or the bad side of the tree of knowledge, that is made apart from Him who is Love becomes self love and is therefore evil—mere humanism. Jesus, as our pattern (the new Adam), did only what He saw the Father doing. He said, "Follow Me…." By that He did not mean just doing what He did. He meant that we were only to do things from being one with Him, from being filled with Him, and only what He is doing in us and through us. It is not Christ helping me but Christ in me that is the hope of glory.

John 17:7-8; 20-23; 26:

> *Now they know that everything You have given Me comes*
> *from You. For I gave them the words You gave Me and they*

accepted them. They knew with certainty that I came from You, and they believed that You sent Me...My prayer is not for them alone. I pray also for those who will believe in Me through their message, that all of them may be one, Father, just as You are in Me and I am in You. May they also be in us so that the world may believe that You have sent Me. I have given them the glory that You gave me, that they may be one as we are one: I in them and You in Me. May they be brought to complete unity to let the world know that You sent Me and have loved them even as You have loved Me...I have made You known to them, and will continue to make You known in order that the love You have for Me may be in them and that I myself may be in them.

So we know where evil began—in the Garden. It was where man chose to advance himself independently of God. Evil is the absence of good and so, the absence of God. Our negative empty self is necessary so that we can be filled with God who is the positive, the only real good and love there is. All else is a shadow and a lie, however real it may seem.

We don't get God—God gets us. We don't get to be good, peaceful, or loving...goodness gets us. He who is peace gets us and He who is love gets us and so we are made one with Him. As the children of God, we too become love, goodness, peace, etc. Joy, peace, and righteousness in the Holy Spirit. That is the plan—all else is negative and evil.

In the Garden of Eden, our ancestors pursued wisdom as if it were something apart from God. All knowledge is nothing without Him. Jesus said, *"I am the way, the truth and I am life. No one comes to the Father except by Me"* (see John 14:6).

Jesus came to make this known to us. He came to make the Father known. Eternal life means knowing Him, the only true God and Jesus whom He sent. He also said, *"...As the Father has sent Me, I am sending you"* (John 20:21). Just as Jesus was the Father to us, we are to be Jesus and the Father to this world. This is the Gospel of the Kingdom: to be Jesus in this world and to draw other lost sons and daughters into the exquisite experience of knowing God in this way.

We go with Him (not He goes with us) who is love living in us. We go into each day with the very authority of His person living in us. We are to take initiative as we listen for His voice and are led by the Spirit. All we are is Jesus. God in us will attract and gather others through our being one with Him. All this by faith and faith alone!

> *But you will receive power when the Holy Spirit comes on you; and you will be My witnesses in Jerusalem, and in all Judea and Samaria, and to the ends of the earth* (Acts 1:8).

> *Therefore go and make disciples of all nations, baptizing them in the name of the Father and of the Son and of the Holy Spirit, and teaching them to obey everything I have commanded you. And surely I am with you always, to the very end of the age* (Matthew 28:19-20).

SOMETHING TO DO

Commit yourself to a life of listening to God—to receiving and responding to His life-giving Word to you. Commit to being His son or daughter and trusting yourself fully to the Father's love and, in faith, obeying all He says.

THE END

OR, IF YOU LIKE,

THE BEGINNING

Additional copies of this book and other
book titles from Destiny Image are
available at your local bookstore.

Call toll-free: 1-800-722-6774.

Send a request for a catalog to:

Destiny Image® Publishers, Inc.
P.O. Box 310
Shippensburg, PA 17257-0310

*"Speaking to the Purposes of God for This
Generation and for the Generations to Come."*

**For a complete list of our titles,
visit us at www.destinyimage.com.**